I need a Shepherd! Though many look to me for leadership, I am profoundly aware that my ministry is only as good as my decisions to follow the One who called me. In the dry lands and dusty fields of present life, I would falter except for the care, loving sustenance, empowering, and direction from my Shepherd. Phyllis Benigas has offered me sheltered meadows, cool drinks, and quiet moments with Him. I am grateful and will cherish her book as I recommend it to others. Indeed, I treasure these *Intimate Moments With the Shepherd*.

—Terry Raburn
District Superintendent
Peninsular Florida Assemblies of God

Phyllis Benigas emerges from a rich background of ministerial and sociological insight. Involved in ministries in churches with her husband, Tom, and presently in association with him as a leading state-wide youth leader, Phyllis has observed firsthand the challenges all of us face in life. Her conclusions are Bible-based and pragmatic. She has also worked alongside me in the increasingly urgent field of world missions. I value both her concept of life and the way she lives it. Her observations in this devotional book will be an inspirational help to every reader.

—Dan Betzer
Senior Pastor, First Assembly of God
Ft. Myers, Florida

We have known Phyllis Benigas for many years, and her book will make you think of more than the Twenty-third Psalm. She shows you that you can be guided through the challenges of life. Phyllis has been an inspiration and guiding force for the youth of Florida and missionaries around the world. The trials of her own life have given her insight for guidance from the Good Shepherd.

—Don Lunsford
Senior Pastor, Faith Assembly of God
St. Petersburg, Florida

Joyce and I read good devotionals every day during our prayer times together. We are anticipating a wonderful compilation of daily spiritual food from a woman of God whom we know really loves the Lord and has been faithful to the kingdom of God through many years. I'm talking about our dear friend and parishioner for a long time, Phyllis Benigas.

—Karl and Joyce Strader
Carpenter's Home Internet Church

Thanks to Phyllis Benigas's masterful sheep photography and beautifully written vignettes, we are poignantly reminded that the Great Shepherd has the answer to life's dilemmas. Reading this book will not only help you reflect and refocus, it will refresh and restore you! It's like a cool drink on a hot day!

—Kristy Dykes
Award-Winning Author & Speaker
www.christianlovestories.blogspot.com

Phyllis has the unique ability to immediately capture readers, hold their attention, and deliver a life lesson straight from her heart. Her writing inspires me to remember God's style is creative, His love is relentless, and His grace has no boundaries. She will touch your heart, and, in the process, bring you face to face with Jesus Christ!

—Randy Brummitt
Senior Pastor, First Assembly of God
Eufaula, Alabama

In a world in which the pace seems increasingly accelerated, with mounting pressures and immense challenges, Phyllis's obedience in sharing the soothing, comforting, and encouraging lessons revealed to her through her quiet times is an invaluable gift to readers. The devotionals contained in these pages are a reminder that we must never lose sight of the fact that we are the sheep and that our Lord is our Shepherd—always leading, guiding, and protecting us from harm's way. The gleaming radiance of the divinely inspired words in *Intimate Moments With the Shepherd* will warm your heart and soothe your soul.

—Susan Benigas
President, AMP It Up for Life, Inc.

Phyllis has been a mentor and inspiration to me. As a pastor's wife, I have always felt safe opening my heart to her words of wisdom and allowing her ministry to speak into my life.

—Christine Ivie
Pastor's Wife, Living Springs Community Church
Bonita Springs, Florida

Phyllis is a treasure! Every time I have the opportunity to hear her speak, I come with my pencil and notepad ready—I can always be sure that I am going to learn some unforgettable lesson! Beyond her words is a tremendous example of what God can do with a life truly submitted to Him. Her ministry has always served as a gentle and loving reminder that the Shepherd loves His sheep.

—Jennifer Spivey
Pastor's Wife, Northland Assembly of God
Cumming, Georgia

INTIMATE MOMENTS *with the* Shepherd

Blessings to you
as you follow
the Shepherd!
Phyllis
Bennett

Intimate Moments with the Shepherd

Phyllis Benigas

Creation House
A Strang Company

INTIMATE MOMENTS WITH THE SHEPHERD
by Phyllis Benigas
Published by Creation House
A Strang Company
600 Rinehart Road
Lake Mary, Florida 32746
www.creationhouse.com

English definitions are from *Webster's New World Dictionary*, 2nd College Edition (New York: William Collins & World Publishing, Inc., 1974), and Word 2003 Thesaurus.

Cover design by Jerry Pomales

Library of Congress Control Number: 2007940828
International Standard Book Number: 978-1-59979-289-7

First Edition

08 09 10 11 12 — 987654321
Printed in the United States of America

*To the two greatest inspirations of my life:
my Heavenly Father and my husband, Tom.
If you know Him and him, you will see their
inspiration on every page.*

ACKNOWLEDGMENTS

MY DEEP APPRECIATION TO:

Tom, my husband of thirty-six years, whose belief in this project has never wavered and whose love for me thrills my heart every day.

My precious mom, Marguerite Annoni, who introduced this questioning three-year-old to the Shepherd so very long ago, as well as hundreds of other souls.

My wonderful children, Amanda and Bryan, Brady and Lacey, who never cease to bless, encourage, and amaze me as they pursue the Lord.

My dear friend and sister-in-law, Susan, who saw the mandate on this book and lovingly pushed and nudged until I could do nothing else but write it.

Countless encouragers, including: Melody Carlson and Donna Nelson (the best sisters ever!), Leona Benigas, Brenda Mack, the Missions Gang (Don and Beverly Lunsford, Juanita and Dean Blackburn, Gloria Jackson, Joe and Margaret Register, Dick and Eva Ludden, Gene and Jeanne Lamay), Randy Brummitt, Tammy Stanley, Laura Hope, Kristy Dykes, Sean Smith, and Christie Ivie.

The wonderful shepherds from around the country who opened their farms and hearts to us and this project.

Barbara Dycus, Allen Quain, Ginny Maxwell, and the great team from Creation House who, with amazing patience and encouragement, enabled me to follow God's leading.

The Lord Jesus, for trusting me with His visual impressions and providing His inspiration for their applications.

Contents

Foreword

As a devotee of devotional books and one who usually reads four of them each day, I approached *Intimate Moments With the Shepherd* with a more than casual interest.

What a wonderful idea to plumb the exhaustless depths and possibilities of our relationship with Jesus as illustrated by the simple example of a shepherd and his sheep. My friend, Phyllis Benigas, tackled this project as she would any other, with exhaustive research and prayerful attention given to each detail.

I've known Phyllis for many years and would place her on my short list of the consistent, godly women who have crossed my path. She brings to this devotional book her own life of devotion as a fervent believer, Christian wife, and mother.

For many years Phyllis has worked faithfully alongside her husband, Tom, as he directs the youth activities for thousands of young people in the Peninsular Florida District of the Assemblies of God. Only eternity could possibly reveal the countless young, confused lives she has rescued and directed away from a path of destruction and pain as she gently pointed them to a loving, caring Shepherd.

The same could be said of her frequent appearances on my Homekeepers television program. As her conversation directs the viewers to Jesus, it is obvious that she knows Him intimately, and her greatest desire is to follow Him as closely as possible. This book will help you do the same.

—Arthelene Rippy
Producer and Host
Homekeepers Television Ministry

INTRODUCTION

"EVERYONE IS LOOKING FOR A SHEPHERD." THIS THOUGHT filled my mind after I read the beloved twenty-third Psalm during my devotional time one morning several years ago. When I realized that God was speaking to me, my simple response was the question, "They are?"

No one had ever asked me how to find a shepherd, but I knew in my heart that everyone was indeed looking for one. My mind was flooded with example after example of man's obvious attempts to find guidance through horoscopes, palm readers, and psychic hotlines, and his more subtle search through the daily consumption of 24/7 news and the vast internet. Everyone is looking for answers, seeking someone or something to guide them through the challenges of life.

During my most intimate moments with the Lord, I began to receive what I call visual impressions of the Good Shepherd and His sheep. These short scenarios displayed the guidance, protection, and loving discipline that the Shepherd provides for the sheep that follow Him. Most of them involved the Shepherd rescuing His sheep from challenging circumstances. I recorded each scenario in my journal because they blessed me on many different levels.

In my devotional time about 8:00 a.m. (EST) on September 11, 2001, I received an especially sobering scenario. Just a short while later, as I continued preparing for the day, I turned on the television set expecting to see Martha Stewart. Instead, I saw the image of the World Trade Center with smoke billowing out near the top of one of the towers. I saw the second plane hit the second tower and realized, with all Americans, that we were under attack.

When the first tower crumbled to the ground, I remembered the scenario I had received from the Lord earlier that morning and realized the similarity to what I had just witnessed. (This devotional is entitled *Victory Over Terror.*) The Lord spoke to my heart and said, "Phyllis, I love you enough to give these impressions just to you, but I want you to know that they are not only for you." In light of the day's events, I realized that everyone is looking for a shepherd.

The only thing I know about four-legged sheep is what the Lord has shown me. However, I do know something about His sheep, having served in ministry alongside my husband the past thirty-seven years, counseling and encouraging the flock. In both the Old and New Testaments, God's followers are compared to sheep. Why? While sheep are considered dumb—a description that is not very flattering—we will see that sheep may more accurately be called *willful,* because they strive to do their own thing, in their own way, and in their own timing. This sounds vaguely familiar. Don't be overly concerned that a few of the sheep in this book do things they should never really do; occasionally we also do things that humans should never really do.

As I was completing the text of this devotional book, something kept gnawing at me—the Lord wanted me to photograph sheep for the book. With "city girl" written all over me, I did my best to ignore this prompting. Eventually, however, I suggested to my husband that we get some sheep pictures and learned that he had already determined in his heart that we needed to do this. The past three years we have traipsed through dozens of sheep pastures and have taken hundreds of sheep pictures. We were blessed over and over as shepherds shared their stories and their sheep. Each visit confirmed that my visual impressions were truly from the Lord.

Like the sheep in my scenarios, we face challenges, sometimes overwhelming, on a daily basis. It is my heartfelt desire that the following devotionals will encourage you when everything seems bleak, that they will correct you when you have lost your way, and that they will instruct you when you don't know what to do. Look no further for a shepherd. We have a Shepherd—the Lord Jesus—to guide us along life's pathway. "We are his people, the sheep of his pasture" (Ps. 100:3). And all we have to do is follow.

Chapter 1

The Road Map

LIFE IS COMPLEX. THERE ARE SO MANY PATHS TO follow and so many different solutions to each problem. The stress of making the right choices in life can be overwhelming and cause us to second-guess each one. Technology has produced the Global Positioning System (GPS), a satellite-guided road map in a box to guide the automobile driver to his destination. How wonderful it would be to have a clearly marked road map from the sky above to guide our lives and leave no guesswork. Oh, that's right, there is!

The Shepherd was leading His flock down a path but stopped when He came to a *Y*. After a while, the sheep became restless. Some started down one path and some down the other. Yet, He waited. A few stayed with the Shepherd, and He smiled at them. Finally, all the sheep but one had started down one of the paths. Still, He waited. The one trusting sheep began stomping his hooves impatiently, wanting to proceed on the journey. Waiting was difficult.

Suddenly, a third path, golden and bright, appeared between the two paths, and the Shepherd motioned for the lone sheep to come with Him. The sheep that had started down the wrong paths only a short time before were able to turn around and join the Shepherd. However, some had traveled too far to observe where the Shepherd was now leading. What became of them? No one knows—except the Shepherd. However, we know the character of the Shepherd, and He will seek them out, calling each one to follow Him.

When we find ourselves agonizing over life's decisions, it is possible that we have lost sight of the Shepherd. The Psalmist David lived with this assurance about our Shepherd:

> You chart the path ahead of me and tell me where to stop and rest. Every moment you know where I am.
>
> —Psalm 139:3, TLB

> You have made known to me the path of life; you will fill me with joy in your presence.
>
> —Psalm 16:11, NIV

It seems logical, then, for us to *wait* for His direction when we come to a *Y* or a *why* in the road. However, we often become impatient to move on or feel pressured to do so.

It is easy to envy the manner in which the Lord led the Israelites to the Promised Land in the book of Exodus. He guided them with a pillar of cloud by day and a pillar of fire by night, and required only that they follow it. Yet somehow these blessed people found it in their hearts to complain about almost everything. (See Exodus 13:20–23.) In our smugness we consider them rude and ungrateful—we would give anything for that pillar to lead us. However, we possess so much more.

Where is our cloud, our pillar of fire, our road map? The Bible, with sixty-six books of guidance and direction, is our road map. It was written expressly for each of us and is an interactive link to heaven—a *live chat* if you will.

"For the word of God is *alive* and powerful" (Heb. 4:12, emphasis added). At the moment, when we most need His guidance—never too early and never too late—the Lord leads us to the very words that will direct our course or encourage our hearts. As we "chat" with Him in prayer, He confirms His Word in our hearts through the Holy Spirit.

Imagine the overwhelming joy in the heart of the one trusting sheep when the third path appeared in all its glory. The *right* path was evident. So it is with us when we face decisions—which job, which house, which church, which friends? We wait, reading God's Word and praying, until our Shepherd reveals a path—perhaps one we did not know existed—that shines brighter and brings *peace* to our hearts. It may not always be the most attractive path, but His mark of *rightness* makes it compelling, "like the first gleam of dawn, which shines ever brighter until the full light of day" (Prov. 4:18).

Chapter 2

Beside the Still Waters

THE JOURNEY OF LIFE, WITH ITS CHALLENGING SITUAtions and difficult people, can be tough. However, the Shepherd provides a place of refuge and healing in our times of desperate need. As the psalmist David said, "He maketh me to lie down in green pastures: he leadeth me beside the still waters. He restoreth my soul" (Ps. 23:2–3, KJV).

Up ahead lay a beautiful field with large, leafy trees and a still, inviting pond. The weary sheep trudged along with the hope of reaching this oasis to stop and rest. Many from the flock were battle-scarred, weak, and bleeding, but they were alive.

Although their journey was not finished, the Shepherd called these walking wounded to come and eat, to lie down, and to be restored. He provided a place where they could be renewed in body, mind, and spirit. The Shepherd was there, of course, because it is His presence that transforms *any* setting into a tranquil place.

Why do we continue walking with our wounds? Injuries, no matter how they are acquired, heal with proper care and with rest. Broken hearts mend with tender loving care and time. Even warriors in the heat of battle must stop to rest and recover from their wounds.

We have lived with some wounds so long that they have become part of our emotional tapestry. People know us by our wounds. Restoration could change our relational dynamics, but we erroneously think that others might not like us any longer. The truth is that they would like us more, and more would like us.

Perhaps we fail to realize that we are wounded because we keep busy applying a salve to our hurts—a salve of denial that keeps them soft and vulnerable, ready to fester from even the slightest bump. Nothing is wrong; everything is fine.

Anger will keep us walking—it energizes. Silver shines,

floors gleam, and windows sparkle when a woman is angry about something. However, after a while anger turns to bitterness, and bitterness is a deadly thing. Harboring bitterness towards those who have wounded us is like shooting ourselves in the foot and expecting the offender to do the limping. We only harm ourselves. The wound goes deeper and becomes more painful.

Regardless of the reason we are walking wounded, it is time to *lie* down in green pastures and *lay* down all those things that have wounded us. It is time to rest beside the still waters and take a break from doctoring our own wounds. It is time to be restored in His presence and no longer ask *why* did this happen? Instead, we must ask God *what* we need to be whole again. Do we need to forgive, forget, trust? The Shepherd is calling us to be restored.

Chapter 3

THE JOY OF RESTORATION

CASUALTIES OF WAR ARE GENERALLY CAUSED BY ENEMY fire. Occasionally, however, soldiers fight the enemy with such zeal and determination that they may make mistakes and inflict unintentional injury or death—friendly fire—on those within their own ranks. This is difficult because it is unexpected—we never think about protecting ourselves from wounds that come from a friend.

It was nightfall and the Shepherd was leading His flock to the fold. Slowing down somewhat, He turned His head to look back over the flock as though He sensed a crisis, and then continued on. The sheep finally reached the fold and darkness fell on them as they hurried through the opening. After securing the gate, the Shepherd walked back up the path and found an injured ewe, accompanied by two sheep that were nudging and encouraging her to continue down the path to the fold.

When the ewe saw the Shepherd, she collapsed, not only from her injury, but also from the painful action that had caused it. In their rush to the safety of the fold, other sheep had pushed her to the side, causing her to fall, and then left her beside the path. She had found it hard to accept that the source of her injury was from within the flock, and her spirit was crushed.

The Shepherd gently stroked the ewe and reassured her that the injury was not fatal, regardless of what had caused it. He told her that the injury to her body would heal, whether she remained on the path or returned to the fold. However, if she did not return to the flock, her spirit may never be restored. With this truth, He guided her along the path back to the fold.

As the injured ewe approached the fold, the zealous sheep that had pushed her aside were stirring at the gate, bleating with joy because she was coming. Some of them were not even aware of the pain they had caused. Oh, how it encouraged the ewe! She would never have known the joy of restoration had she not continued on the Shepherd's path to the fold.

Though they are normally considered docile, sheep that are on a mission, as any shepherd knows, are a force to reckon with. Whether they are on a run for food or shelter, or fighting for their lives, they will put their heads down and *go*, and pity the poor sheep that gets in their path. People will do the same. In a culture where aggressive behavior earns the job, wins the title, and defeats the enemy, collateral damage is certain to occur. Even though Solomon declared that "wounds from a sincere friend are better than many kisses from an enemy" (Prov. 27:6), the injuries they cause are unexpected and, therefore, even more hurtful.

When we find ourselves caught by friendly fire, we are tempted to collapse from the injustice of it all. However, it is important to remember that others have also suffered it. When David's own son, Absalom, turned on him and tried to take his kingdom, that had to hurt. In Psalm 55:12–13, the wounded psalmist wrote, "It is not an enemy who taunts me—I could bear that. It is not my foes who so arrogantly insult me—I could have hidden from them. Instead, it is you—my equal, my companion and close friend."

Jesus suffered this pain. Luke 4:29 records that people in His hometown wanted to kill Jesus. "Jumping up, they mobbed him and forced him to the edge of the hill on which the town was built. They intended to push him over the cliff." Jesus understands our pain. We are in good company.

When we find ourselves caught by friendly fire, forgiveness is our only recourse, if we desire to be restored. Forgiveness is a three-step process: forgive, forget, and trust. We *forgive* those zealous sheep, who in their pursuit of their own agendas may not even realize the pain they have caused. Jesus offered the ultimate example of forgiveness as He suffered on the cross, "Father, forgive these people...for they don't know what they are doing" (Luke 23:34, TLB). We *forget* by refusing to rehearse the pain over and over again—is it really a scenario we want to relive? The ewe had to leave the place of injury and move on to discover restoration.

And *trust* is an act that results from loving again—loving those who have wounded us regardless of their intent, regardless of their awareness, regardless of their remorse. Love is the one thing that will protect us, too, when we hurt others.

In the words of Paul to the Corinthians:

> Love is patient and kind. Love is not jealous or boastful or proud or rude. Love does not demand its own way. Love is not irritable, and *it keeps no record of when it has been wronged*. It does not rejoice about injustice but rejoices whenever the truth wins out. Love never gives up, never loses faith, is always hopeful, and endures through every circumstance.
>
> —1 Corinthians 13:4–7, emphasis added

Oh, the joy of restoration!

Chapter 4
Through the Valley

Even though I walk through the valley of the shadow of death, I will fear no evil, for you are with me.

—Psalm 23:4, NIV

It is fearsome to think about a valley of death without the word *shadow* in it. A shadow cannot exist where there is no *light,* and, thankfully, our Shepherd is the Light who walks with us through the valley. How comforting it is to know that we will pass into eternal life in the presence of the Shepherd!

As the Shepherd sat on the ground, an elderly sheep lay beside Him, its head resting on His thigh. They had been inseparable in life, and it was only natural that they would be together now when this cherished sheep was dying. The Shepherd's gentle strokes comforted and soothed the old sheep, and it lifted its leg to rest on the Shepherd as if to say it knew He was present. The other sheep stood around in a somber mood, completely silent, none of them eating or moving.

As the old sheep took its last breath, the Shepherd's face glistened with tears, and He gently laid the dear one's head down. They had been together for such a long time, always faithful to each other through many great moments and some not-so-great moments. The Shepherd and the others would mourn, but they would move on. The beloved sheep would want it this way. There were still many lost sheep to find.

Death is not a stopping point in the valley, but a passage through it. It is one of the many things we experience on our way to eternity. For those who follow the Shepherd, it is difficult to imagine walking through death's valley without Him. It would be a fearful thing to approach this valley without His comforting words and soothing touch, without the hope of an eternal future with Him on the other side.

God's heart is revealed in Psalm 116:15, where it tells us that the Lord's loved ones are precious to Him and it *grieves*

Him when they die. He is acquainted with our grief and has experienced our loss, and this comforts us. But why would the Lord grieve the death of one of His precious ones when they will now be together for eternity? Perhaps it is roughly similar to the feelings a father experiences on his daughter's wedding day. He has loved, nurtured, provided for, and protected her from birth, and now on this day, his role has changed. Tears are shed, and they happily embrace this new and different loving relationship.

So it is with the Lord. We meet Him at the foot of the cross as our *Savior* and walk through life with Him as our *Shepherd* who loves, nurtures, sustains, and protects us on life's journey. We share many great moments, and some not-so-great moments with Him. When we walk through death's valley, tears may be shed over the end of what we have experienced together on earth. However, we will embrace a new and different loving relationship on the other side. We will find ourselves at the foot of His throne, worshiping Him in person as our *King*. We will join in the anthem of all creation, "Blessing and honor and glory and power belong to the One sitting on the throne and to the *Lamb* forever and ever" (Rev. 5:13, emphasis added).

When someone we love moves on to this glorious position at His throne, we grieve our loss. Yet, we will continue through this life with our Shepherd, finding many others who need a Savior, a Shepherd, and a King. Our loved ones would want it this way.

Chapter 5

More Than a Walking Stick

The Shepherd's staff is significantly more than a mere walking stick. Its position in the Shepherd's hand provides direction for the flock. Its length provides a safe means of warding off predators. The intentional crook is ideal for rescuing sheep from harm's way. Yes, the Shepherd's staff comforts the sheep.

Rain and fog made the journey difficult as the flock followed the Shepherd through a wide, rocky valley. Without warning, a wall of water came crashing through the valley, separating some of the sheep from the Shepherd as they ran to safety. They could see the Shepherd and the other sheep, but now a body of water stood between them. However, having followed Him for quite some time, they knew He wanted them to hold steady because of the way He held His staff.

The isolated sheep waited with peaceful hearts, their eyes fixed on the Shepherd. They were sure He would deliver them because He always had. As they focused on the Shepherd, they failed to notice that the waters had subsided, providing a natural path straight to Him. When He raised His staff, they realized it was safe to advance toward Him. All the sheep safely joined the Shepherd and continued on their way in unity, pondering in their hearts what had happened.

If the rocky terrain was not challenging enough, rain and fog had settled into the valley to diminish the sheep's visibility. Thus, the wall of water came as a surprise to them and brought division. Unfortunately, this is a possible scenario within any group of people, whether families, churches, businesses, nations.

At times, bumps in the road captivate our attention and slow us down, various elements of life cause confusion, and before we know it, we have division. A job transfer uproots a family and the adjustment is difficult for the children. Church members disagree on a building project. Workers and management cannot come to terms on benefits. A nation is divided on the legitimacy of war. We did not ask for division, we do not want it, we do not like it; however, we do have it. *Where* we look for the solution is what determines the outcome.

The isolated sheep remained peaceful and hopeful because they focused their attention on the Shepherd, not on the water that divided them. Watching the water would have brought anxiety. Instead, they followed the exhortation of Hebrews 12:1–2: "Let us run with endurance the race that God has set before us. We do this by *keeping our eyes on Jesus,* on whom our faith depends from start to finish" (emphasis added).

As they looked at the Shepherd's staff, they saw it as an object of comfort. Psalm 23:4 declares, "Your rod and your staff protect and comfort me." The staff was an extension of the Shepherd's intentions, and its position dictated to the sheep how they were to move. The staff never moved on its own volition. When the passage was safe, the staff was used to signal a safe advance for the watchful sheep.

The use of the Shepherd's staff may be more familiar to us than we may think. We should view our authorities, the leadership over us, as an extension of the Lord's intentions for us. When the Lord provides a solution to our separation, He will use our leaders—parents, pastors, employers, and presidents—to signal our safe passage.

God is the originator of spiritual authority. Leadership is submitted responsibility, and submitted authorities are intended by God to be a comfort to us. However, any authority that moves according to its own volition would be an object completely unlike His authority. When we question our authority's submission to God, we are not comforted, and we can respond in one of three ways. We can submit to the authority, rebel, or step away.

Submission to spiritual authority, even during times of division, is what the Bible promotes from Genesis to Revelation. Hebrews 13:17 encourages, "Obey your spiritual leaders and do what they say. Their work is to watch over your souls, and they know they are accountable to God. Give them reason to do this with joy and not with sorrow. That would certainly not be for your benefit."

Yes, submission is the way God wants us to respond. If our authority is in error, God will deal with that person; if we rebel, God will deal with us. Some situations allow us the option of just leaving. If we choose to do so, we are wise to collect our belongings and leave—quietly, alone. However, when we do this, we often just postpone the inevitable and meet a similar situation in the future.

The once divided flock was brought back together because the sheep who were separated from the Shepherd kept their eyes on Him and His staff. In Romans 15:5–6, Paul exhorted the Romans to live in unity:

> May God, who gives this patience and encouragement, help you live in complete harmony with each other [each with the attitude of Christ Jesus towards the other]. . . . Then all of you can join together with one voice, giving praise and glory to God, the Father of our Lord Jesus Christ.

Unity! It's music to the Shepherd's ears.

Chapter 6

THE DILEMMA OF DISTRACTIONS

A DISTRACTION IS NOT NECESSARILY BAD. VARIOUS forms of entertainment may distract us from the severity of pain, and hobbies serve as a wonderful remedy to boredom. However, a distraction is also capable of disrupting our focus and pulling us off track. Horse trainers face this dilemma, and they have developed blinders that cup around the eyes of their horses to narrow their field of vision and keep the horse focused on the course before it. We, by our consistent choices to focus on the Shepherd, can overcome distractions.

Two sheep had been following closely behind the Shepherd for several days. While the ewe was content with their choice to follow the Shepherd, she was constantly being pulled off the path by the ram, which was easily distracted by things alongside the path. The couple fell farther and farther behind the Shepherd, and although they could still see Him, they could no longer hear what He was saying to the flock.

Each distraction was pleasurable, but the ewe could not fully enjoy it because she was trying to keep her eye on the Shepherd. He and the flock had now become only a speck on the horizon, and she knew she had to catch up with them. She took off running with hope that the ram would follow, and he did—for a while. However, because there were so many distractions and it was exhausting to run so hard, he soon lagged even farther behind.

Through much effort, the ewe finally reached the Shepherd, alone and with great sadness. She knew her companion had yielded to yet another pursuit along the way. The wise Shepherd, sensing her unhappiness, walked with her for many miles and spoke words of comfort to her. The ewe knew she was where she belonged.

After our enemy's many failed attempts to *destroy* our lives, he will, at the very least, make an effort to *distract* us. The wide variety of distractions—grassy clumps, flowering meadows, and mountain streams along the path—are extremely attractive to us if we focus on our own desires rather than the Shepherd. It is no wonder that Jesus, in Mark 8:34, TLB, encouraged His disciples, "If any of you wants to be my follower…you must *put aside* your own pleasures and shoulder your cross, and follow me closely" (emphasis added).

In our walk with the Shepherd, we often find that we enjoy the company of someone who, like the ram, is enticed by everything life has to offer. As it was with the ewe, this presents a constant struggle in our endeavor to follow the Lord. In 2 Corinthians 6:14–15 Paul cautions us, "Don't team up with those who are unbelievers. How can righteousness be a partner with wickedness? How can light live with darkness? What harmony can there be between Christ and the devil? How can a believer be a partner with an unbeliever?" Even when a wanderer claims to be a follower, he really isn't one until he *follows*. Proverbs 12:26 advises, "The godly give good advice to their friends; the wicked lead them astray."

The ewe reached her Shepherd by running and not looking back, by keeping her eyes on the speck on the horizon and not looking aside at the scenery. Wistfully looking back on our past is a distraction. A longing look back proved fatal for Lot's wife as she ran from the evil city of Sodom in Genesis 19, and she turned into a pillar a salt. How can we avoid this?

The answer of Paul in Hebrews 12 is:

> Let us strip off every weight that slows us down, especially the sin that so easily trips us up. And let us run with endurance the race that God has set before us. *We*

> *do this by keeping our eyes on Jesus,* on whom our faith depends from start to finish.
>
> —Hebrews 12:1–2, emphasis added

It was no surprise that the Shepherd knew how to comfort the ewe as she walked with Him. He, too, loved the ram and was saddened by his unwillingness to follow Him. She was comforted in the knowledge that her Shepherd will continue to look for him, call to him, and joyfully receive him when he finds his way back to Him—where he belongs.

Chapter 7
GUIDED STEPS

POOR CHOICES, WILLFUL DISOBEDIENCE, AND, MOST DEFInitely, serving a different god can lead us to a place of misery. At such times, we know deep within our hearts that we must find the path back to God. But have we gone too far too long? Have we burned too many bridges to return to God? How could we ever forget the parable of the lost sheep!

A sheep had wandered away from the flock and was now isolated on the edge of a rocky cliff, frozen with fear. It was not clear how the sheep had come to experience such danger. Perhaps it had followed the enticement of better grazing; more than likely it was a case of gradually moving away from the flock, away from the Shepherd.

The Shepherd followed the sheep's mournful cry and was relieved when He looked up and found it perched on the cliff's edge. Undaunted by the sheep's precarious position, the Shepherd threw a rope around its neck to help it down to level ground. However, the sheep resisted and pulled back with its neck, fearful because one wrong step on the rocky cliff could prove fatal. Misguided steps had brought it to the cliff, and it may be safer just to stay there. The sheep earnestly wanted to be with the Shepherd but it was afraid of the journey back to Him.

The Shepherd continued to gently tug, urging the sheep to trust Him and take that first step to Him. A stronger tug forced the sheep to take one small step without consequence, then another, and another. The going was tough at times, but not fatal. With the Shepherd's patient guidance, the resistant sheep finally found itself safe at His feet, filled with overwhelming peace.

The Shepherd's determination to save the sheep may best be explained by the parable of Jesus in Matthew 18:12, "If a man owns a hundred sheep, and one of them wanders away, will he not leave the ninety-nine on the hills and go to look for the one that wandered off?" (NIV). Much to our amazement, the Lord is always willing to search for us and restore us regardless of our position or circumstance.

However, our apprehension and fear often hinder our reunion with the Shepherd. "Why would God be willing to take me back after all I have done to hurt Him?" "What will I be required to give up if I follow after Him?" "What will others say?" "Will they exclude me because of my past?" As the Shepherd did with the sheep, God sometimes forces that first small step back to Him by allowing us to experience situations that turn our thoughts to Him. With each guided step back to Him, our hindering questions fade away. And when we finally find ourselves safe at His feet filled with overwhelming peace, we wonder why we resisted Him so long.

Chapter 8

Complete Trust

FOLLOWING THE SHEPHERD DOES NOT SECURE A LIFE FREE from obstacles and trials, but following Him does provide the means to overcome hindrances. Complete trust in the Lord moves Him to not only strengthen us during difficult times, but to also perform miracles on our behalf.

The Shepherd and sheep found themselves looking down upon a beautiful valley that was lush with vegetation and had a cool stream. At first the downhill slope to the valley was easy to maneuver, but the descent grew increasingly difficult. When He reached a plateau, the Shepherd walked along it, searching for the path that He knew existed. The grade appeared to be too steep in every direction, and the path downward was hidden from the sheep. Then, however, it appeared out of nowhere, a hidden staircase that nature had carved out of the rock.

The flock proceeded down the mountain to graze in the beautiful valley, and the Shepherd cooled His feet in the stream. Looking back up the mountain, it seemed impossible that the sheep could have traversed it. No hidden stairs, no path could be seen except by the guidance of the wise Shepherd who has all heaven and earth in His hands. The sheep reached this special place because they trusted Him.

In the book of Exodus, the children of Israel found themselves wedged between the Red Sea and the Egyptian army with no visible way of escape. (See Exodus 14.) David expressed their deliverance best when he wrote:

> When the Red Sea saw you, O God, its waters looked and trembled! The sea quaked to its very depths.... Your road led through the sea, your pathway through the mighty waters—*a pathway no one knew was there!* You

> led your people along that road like a flock of sheep with
> Moses and Aaron as their shepherds.
>
> —Psalm 77:16, 19–20, emphasis added

Skeptics insist that the waters of the Red Sea were shallow and that a miracle did not occur. However, their argument begs an equally miraculous event—the advancing mighty Egyptian army perished in just a few inches of water. The biblical narrative is true. God saved the Israelites and enabled them to fulfill their destiny.

We may have a vision that appears unattainable. We may find ourselves walking back and forth on a plateau, looking for a path to reach our goal. It may be humanly impossible, but if it is a God-given goal, He has *ten thousand* different ways to attain it. We need to trust Him for just *one*.

Chapter 9

SILVER LININGS

WHILE A PARADE OF ANTS OR A SWARM OF BEES ARE a nuisance at any picnic, the real show stopper is the thunderstorm. As the threatening clouds develop, the wary picnickers choke down their hamburgers and get ready to run for cover because the party is surely over. However, a careful observation of those clouds could possibly change their outlook from party *over* to party momentarily *delayed*. So often an ever-present beaming sun, only temporarily hidden by the imposing cloud, is lining the cloud with an iridescent glow and a promise of sunny skies ahead. We just need to look past the cloud and see the silver lining!

The sheep always enjoyed being in the meadow with its abundant vegetation, and they were reluctant to heed the Shepherd's call to move on. After guiding them through a narrow passage that time had cut through the rocks, He led them onto a rocky, difficult terrain. The sheep clearly found this objectionable and voiced their opposition in noisy bleating. This was not what they wanted, but they obeyed.

It was difficult to walk on the dark, barren terrain; yet as the sheep moved across it they discovered something. Shooting up amongst the rocks were the most tender, delicious sprouts of grass they had ever tasted. They reveled in this unexpected feast in an unexpected place. And when the Shepherd once again called them to move on, they were reluctant to leave.

Walking from the bountiful meadow to the barren rocks did not appear to be a good day for the flock. We can understand this because some of us have walked the barren path of losing a treasured spouse or never embracing a precious newborn. Or perhaps we have experienced dark days of illness or poverty and found ourselves bleating our objections in tear-filled pain. All we recognize are mountainous black clouds—until we see that first sparkle of the silver lining at the edge of the cloud, that first blade of grass poking through the rocks.

Imagine the day when the Virgin Mary discovered that she would soon be pregnant. No doubt she would have preferred being barren over being an unmarried pregnant teenager. However, she valued life over convenience. Her ability to see beyond the cloud of shame and rejection to the beautiful silver lining of redemption for all mankind was evident when she sang:

> Oh, how I praise the Lord. How I rejoice in God my Savior! For he took notice of his lowly servant girl, and now generation after generation forever shall call me blest of God.
>
> —Luke 1:46–48, TLB

The sweet grasses that come from our barren places may not be what we expect or even desire, but they are evidence that God does amazingly well when all is barren and empty. Genesis 1:1–2 introduces the story of creation and says, "In the beginning God created the heavens and the earth. The earth was formless and empty, and darkness covered the deep waters." Six days later, our universe was completed.

Can we trust God with our barrenness, our emptiness, our lack? When we focus beyond things of temporal value to blessings of eternal value, we will discover an unexpected feast in an unexpected place. Our Shepherd, Mary's silver lining, will lead us from the place of barrenness to the land of fruitfulness.

Chapter 10
NO WORRIES

Worry does not empty tomorrow of its sorrow; it empties today of its strength.[1]

THESE INSIGHTFUL WORDS, WHICH CAME FROM THE heart of Corrie ten Boom, a survivor of the German concentration camps of World War II, bear witness to a lesson she learned about accepting God's care instead of worrying and assuming His responsibility for her. Worry is a dreadful thing. It consumes our thoughts, affects our actions, and never accomplishes anything. It almost always comes from taking up responsibility that is not ours to carry, and it leaves when we relinquish that responsibility by trusting the One to whom it does belong.

One of the Shepherd's faithful lead sheep was standing apart from the grazing flock, surveying the unfamiliar pasture for a glimpse of the Shepherd. Its duty was to set an example of following His every move, and because the sheep was unable to see the Shepherd, its stance became rigid with concern. Perhaps the Shepherd was searching for a lost sheep or for new grazing land. In His absence, someone had to care for the flock and protect it from danger. As the reality of this responsibility weighed on the sheep, its muscles tensed and its stomach knotted.

What was only a matter of minutes seemed like hours to the sheep. When it could no longer stand under the strain, the sheep spotted the Shepherd resting on a nearby hillside. It had been so focused on the negative possibilities that could have occurred that it did not realize the Shepherd had been present all along. As the Shepherd came and encircled the sheep in His comforting arms, its muscles relaxed.

The diligent sheep failed to realize that the Shepherd had not assigned it His role as protector of the flock; if He had, He would have given it all the preparation it needed to fulfill the task. While the Shepherd may not have been visible to this sheep, His presence was there, protecting and caring for the flock. The sheep lost its awareness of His presence when it assumed a responsibility it was not given.

This sounds very familiar. When we assume the responsibilities that have been given to a spouse, parent, or employer, we begin to worry and fret because we have not been equipped nor given the authority to handle them. Tension mounts, we suffer physical stress, and, in time, we collapse in exhaustion.

Even more critical is our action of assuming the responsibility of the Shepherd, for He has never called us to be God. When we worry about the provision of our safety and health, our food, our home, our future, or anything, we are assuming His role. Unbelievable! Although we might expect Him to smite us for this, He comes to us with His great mercy as we relinquish control. He encircles us with His great, great love and comforts us.

The Good Shepherd said it best when He taught:

> I tell you not to worry about everyday life—whether you have enough food and drink, or enough clothes.... Can all your worries add a single moment to your life?... Your heavenly Father already knows all your needs.... Seek the Kingdom of God above all else, and live righteously, and he will give you everything you need.
>
> —Matthew 6:25–33

This is Christ's prescription for a life of no worries.

Chapter 11

INFINITELY SIGNIFICANT

IT IS HARD TO COMPREHEND THAT GOD, WHO CREATED and controls the entire universe, would be mindful of insignificant me. David, God's special friend, evidently felt this way when he asked:

> When I consider your heavens, the work of your fingers,
> the moon and the stars, which you have set in place,

> what is man that you are mindful of him, the son of man that you care for him?
>
> —Psalm 8:3–4, NIV

A lamb stood at the feet of the Shepherd and looked up into the face of his towering Leader who seemed to reach into the heavens. Although it seemed impossible for the Shepherd to focus on one so small, the lamb felt as if the eyes of the Shepherd were spotlights shining down on it in the midst of the hundreds of surrounding sheep. At that moment of recognition, the Shepherd reached down, picked up the lamb, and placed it on a nearby ridge.

From this lofty height, the sheep viewed what seemed to be the entire earth in all its majesty. It also viewed what appeared to be an unending sea of sheep following the Shepherd. As the lamb saw all this, the Shepherd asked it, "If I am able to create this and watch over it so that nothing is lacking, will I not be able to care for you?"

Sometimes we just need to change our perspective. Instead of focusing on how small and insignificant we are, we need to see how huge and awesome God is. The psalmist wrote, "The Lord looks down from heaven and sees the whole human race. From His throne He observes all who live on the earth. He made their hearts, so He understands everything they do" (Ps. 33:13–15). Even when we do not understand ourselves, He does; and He directs us according to His understanding.

While we may not comprehend all of the "omni's" of God—His omnipotence, omniscience, and omnipresence—

the measure of faith that exists in our hearts enables us to believe that God is all-powerful, all-knowing, and all-present, capable to see us just where we are. Debilitating emotions such as blinding hatred, paralyzing fear, or a proud heart may suppress our faith. But, faith is still present, waiting for a simple act of trust in God to awaken it.

When faith is awakened in us, God lights the path to our destiny regardless of our obscure surroundings. David, the most humble of shepherds, killed the giant Goliath; later, after defeating all his enemies, he sang praises to God, "O Lord, you are my lamp. The Lord lights up my darkness" (2 Sam. 22:29). God's light enabled a stuttering fugitive named Moses to deliver the Israelites from Egyptian bondage. His light empowered Gideon, the least in his family and from Israel's smallest tribe, to rescue the nation from the destructive Midianites. And the lowly Mary, who bore the Savior, the Light of all mankind, came from Nazareth, a town that was considered unable to produce anything good.

We become infinitely significant when God's spotlight shines on us.

Chapter 12

FAULTY FEELINGS

A POPULAR SONG FROM YEARS AGO DECLARED THAT IF something feels right, it can't be wrong. Unfortunately, it can. What we may *feel* is the very best path for us, may actually bring much heartache. Occasionally our Shepherd allows reality to wake us up to this fact.

In response to the persistent bleating of one little lamb, the Shepherd reached down and playfully petted its head. The lamb grabbed the Shepherd's cloak with its teeth and, with surprising strength, began pulling Him down a path of its own choosing. Apparently it saw something too inviting to miss and was sure the Shepherd would agree if He would only come. The lamb was wise enough to not venture out alone, but it thought that it could influence the Shepherd's direction.

However, this was not going to happen. With a hard tug, the Shepherd pulled His cloak away from the lamb and proceeded down *His* path, calling to the lamb to follow Him. The lamb remained where it was and stood firmly, resolute in its act of self-will. Again, the Shepherd called, and the lamb responded with a stomp. Then, from the bushes behind the lamb came a great roar that sent it flying to the feet of the Shepherd. With a smile on His face, His staff in His hand, and the little lamb at His side, the Shepherd continued on His path.

It is not uncommon for any of us to try to change the mind of God when some person, place, or thing is so enticing and would make us *feel* so good. Surely our loving Heavenly Father would grant us our heart's desire. Thus, we try to convince, manipulate, or even bribe Him to give us that relationship, that house, or that new car. He moves on, but we stay. Because of His great mercy He calls one more time, and eventually we learn that the would-be relationship was abusive, the house had termites, or the car was a lemon. If we have the sense of the little lamb, we run to the Shepherd when He calls us, and we follow His lead.

Some may argue that because God created us with emotions, they can be trusted to guide us along the path. However, while our feelings may be the result of goodness and peace, they may also stem from selfishness and an unforgiving heart. Will a roller coaster ride of feelings keep us safe from the menace behind the roar? Solomon cautioned, "Guard your heart above all else, for it determines the course of your life" (Prov. 4:23). It is so important that we follow a course based on what God has revealed as truth, not our unsound emotions.

Perhaps David was struggling with the pull of his feelings when he prayed

> Show me the right path, O LORD; point out the road for me to follow. Lead me by your truth and teach me, for you are the God who saves me. All day long I put my hope in you. Remember, O LORD, your compassion and unfailing love, which you have shown from long ages past. Do not remember the rebellious sins of my youth. Remember me in the light of your unfailing love, for you are merciful, O LORD.
>
> —Psalm 25:4–7

As we walk along the path with the Shepherd, we will learn to avoid the perils of following the adage, "If it feels good, do it." We will learn to pray as David prayed, "Show me the path where I should walk, O Lord!" (Ps. 25:4).

Chapter 13

ADVENTUROUS FAITH

OUR FAST-PACED LIVES MAY CATAPULT US INTO OPPORTUNITIES or relationships so quickly that we find ourselves paralyzed with fear and trepidation and wondering what to do. Recognizing how God is leading and calling us will help us walk through the open doors He has set before us.

There was great excitement as the Shepherd hurried His sheep to view a place He had chosen for them to enjoy. The pace was so quick that He had to slow down the lead sheep before they reached the point of the impending cliff where they gazed on a bountiful valley below them, filled with tender young herbs. Yes, the flock was in a somewhat precarious position and dependent on the Shepherd's faithful guidance. However, the sheep had learned to trust Him regardless of the adventure—all except one sheep.

When the Shepherd beckoned the flock to move on to this choice grazing pasture, He spotted the frightened sheep. Paralyzed with fear of what could have happened if it had gone over the cliff and of what might happen if it stayed near the cliff's edge, it could not move. It was as if the dazed sheep had forgotten that the trustworthy Shepherd had brought it to this incredible point.

Standing a considerable length away, the Shepherd called over and over again for the sheep to come, to follow Him. Finally, after much coaxing, the sheep ran to the Shepherd and collapsed at His feet. The Shepherd could have easily gone to the sheep, picked him up and carried him safely in His arms away from the cliff. But if He had, how would the sheep have learned to overcome its fear with *trust*—trust in the One who brought it to that point?

God may lead us to a place of leadership, an incredible task, or possibly a ministry opportunity for which we feel completely inadequate. He loves that. He knows that we, in our inadequacy, will be forced to rely on His guidance and direction. However, we may be so completely overwhelmed by God's open door that fear grips and paralyzes us, making it impossible for us to move through the door.

Inadequate, fearful, paralyzed—this is most certainly how Moses felt the day God chose him to free the Israelites from captivity in Egypt. Even God speaking from a burning bush did not help his apprehension. Moses cried out with a plea we understand, "Lord, please! Send anyone else" (Exod. 4:13). After much coaxing by God, Moses moved away from the fear of this daunting task to victory by trusting in the One who called him to it.

We can be encouraged by King David's admonition to young Solomon, who was destined to build the Holy Temple of God:

> Be strong and courageous, and do the work. Do not be afraid or discouraged, for the LORD God, my God, is with you. He will not fail you or forsake you.
>
> —1 Chronicles 28:20, NIV

As we follow our Shepherd, we may suddenly find ourselves in a dangerous position near the edge of a cliff. Instead of reacting with fear, we must run to Him with all our lack, trusting Him as the One who brought us to this point. The Lord God, our God, is with us.

Chapter 14
FINE DINING

HUNGER IS THE BODY'S WAY OF TELLING US IT IS TIME to eat and nourish ourselves. We may become irritable when time restraints, health problems, or anything keeps us from satisfying our hunger, and we will find a way to overcome any obstacle to receiving nutrition. In the same manner, spiritual hunger is the Spirit's way of letting us know it is time to nourish the soul. It motivates us to receive David's invitation, "Taste and see that the LORD is good" (Ps. 34:8, NIV).

Many from the flock were surrounding the Shepherd who held a cloth bag filled with special feed He had handpicked for all the sheep that closely followed Him. The Shepherd was showering them with the feed, more than they could possibly eat. They had great satisfaction and peace.

However, other sheep in the flock were grazing far from the Shepherd, eating whatever they could find to satisfy their hunger. Because of their poor eyesight and the fog that had rolled in, their view of the Shepherd was diminished, and they could not see what He was providing. They were not experiencing the satisfaction and peace of the sheep closest to the Shepherd, and they began focusing on their lack, moaning with irritation and frustration. If only they could see what was available to them beyond the veil of the fog! Then their hunger would be satisfied.

As we follow the Lord we may have times when our view of Him becomes diminished. We are hungry for all that He has for us, but something prevents us from receiving it. We may attend a church service and sense that something special is happening in the lives of others; yet we may be untouched, unable to even distinguish what we are missing. Perhaps the sermon seems too shallow, too long, too boring or the music too slow, too fast, too loud. We may think it would be easier to worship if the carpet were not so blue.

When we are in this condition, we are tempted to become irritable. We begin to think that no one cares about us. Solomon warned, "A wise person is hungry for knowledge, while the fool feeds on trash" (Prov. 15:14). What "trash" has diminished our ability to see the Shepherd clearly? What is preventing us from moving in close and receiving His wonderful blessings and special gifts? If we have broken one of the Ten Commandments, we are usually aware of this disconnect. However, it is likely something more subtle—pride, jealousy, fear, judging others, neglecting Him—veiled offenses that are visible only to Him and us.

Like the hungry sheep, we need to realize that the Shepherd is in our midst, providing all we need to be filled to overflowing. If we are hungry and irritable, it may be time to clear the air with Him by repenting of our offenses. We will experience great satisfaction and peace as we are filled—abundantly filled—to overflowing. And we will join our voices with the testimony of Psalm 145:15–16, NIV, "The eyes of all look to you, and you give them their food at the proper time. You open your hand and satisfy the desires of every living thing." Now that's fine dining!

Chapter 15

FALSE CONFIDENCE

IT IS DIFFICULT TO UNDERSTAND HOW WE MAY BE FAITH-fully following God one moment and in the next moment, find ourselves in the middle of a mess we have caused. Yes, it hardly seems plausible—but it is.

The young sheep was running and jumping carelessly as it followed the Shepherd along the path. It had a certain false confidence because of the Shepherd's offered protection, so the rest of the flock was not surprised when the sheep tumbled down a small hill into a briar patch. It struggled to get out, but every movement seemed to drive the thorns deeper into its flesh and cause greater pain.

Eventually, the merciful Shepherd came to rescue the sheep and slowly removed one thorny branch at a time. During the process, which seemed to take forever, He admonished it to not only follow Him, but to diligently keep its eye on the path ahead. When the lesson was over, the young sheep understood why and how to be a more careful follower.

We have watched world-renowned evangelists, who have led thousands to the Shepherd, take a downward turn that impacts the world. In response, we wonder how a good and godly individual can suffer such obvious failure. "How foolish!" we think. "I would never do such a thing." It is *that* moment when we start to take the wrong turn. Perhaps that is why Solomon cautioned:

> Look straight ahead, and fix your eyes on what lies before you. Mark out a straight path for your feet; stay on the safe path. Don't get sidetracked; keep your feet from following evil.
>
> —Proverbs 4:25–27

Following the Lord brings such peace and confidence to us that our familiarity with it may cause us to forget the Source of it. We become a little careless at first, but we are sure that it won't matter because we would never leave the path. Soon, we jump around from one little offense to another—missing our personal moments with the Shepherd, taking a long second look at one of God's creations, or borrowing someone else's resources. Then, we take the tumble. At first we try to get out of the mess on our own, but it just seems to get more painful.

Before long, the merciful Lord comes and slowly removes the barbs. Sometimes it is a long, painful process back to wholeness, but hopefully we learn much from it. However, the flock will more than likely include observers who think, "How foolish! I would never do such a thing." Let us heed Paul's warning, "If you think you are standing strong, be careful, for you, too, may fall into the same sin" (1 Cor. 10:12).

Chapter 16

A Full Quiver

A quiver is a container that holds arrows. A full quiver may be somewhat crowded and burdensome to carry. Yet, as Psalm 127:3–5 teaches:

> Children are a gift from the Lord; they are a reward from him. Children born to a young man are like arrows in a warrior's hand. How joyful is the man whose quiver is full of them!

A weary ewe was following the Shepherd with her family in tow. Her task of caring for her own was overwhelming at times, and she carried tremendous responsibilities that only a parent can truly understand. She gently pulled her youngest lamb by the ear, helping it to keep pace with her. It was too young to understand why they traveled and too small to see who they followed.

As time passed, an opening in the moving flock enabled the lamb to fix its eye on the Shepherd, and as if drawn like a magnet, it ran to Him and tugged on His garment. The loving Shepherd, always pleased to show His affection, cradled the lamb in His arms and spoke of great things that the mother had never even heard.

The cares and concerns of raising a child can be overwhelming for parents, and each additional child increases the load. It is not a matter of possessing enough love for each child, but the added responsibilities associated with expressing that love. Scripture offers the encouragement that we are not alone in this task. In his message of comfort to God's people, the prophet Isaiah said that God "tends his flock like a shepherd: He gathers the lambs in His arms and carries them close to His heart; he gently leads those that have young" (Isa. 40:11, NIV). We are not alone in our parenting!

As parents, we are like an archer who holds arrows in his quiver. He removes them, one by one, determines the direction they should go, and sends them forth to accomplish his will and fulfill their destinies. In a similar way, we hold our children, protecting and caring for them, until the day they fix their eyes on the Lord. He reveals His will to them and then sends them out to fulfill their destinies.

At times our home may be crowded and the load burdensome, but this is where our happiness lies. We are the *holders* of children God has created to fulfill His will on earth—to accomplish great things of which we may not be aware. How painful it must be for Him when a mother chooses to destroy a life that He is watching over so lovingly in the womb, planning every moment. (See Psalm 139:15–16.) How thrilling it must be for Him when we realize, with great happiness, that He has entrusted us with the responsibility of holding something so precious to Him, regardless of the cost to us.

Do you have a full quiver? Smile, be happy. He is.

Chapter 11

AN AWESOME RESPONSIBILITY

PARENTING IS AN AWESOME RESPONSIBILITY. OUR choices and actions have both an immediate and long-term influence on the young lives we are leading. When life's storms assault our families, we will be assured of safety if we follow the Shepherd closely and follow His direction.

The Shepherd looked off into the distance and saw a fast, whirling storm approaching the flock. The sheep, too, sensed impending danger as animals so often do, and began to panic. Those *close* to the Shepherd waited for His command, but many sheep did what seemed reasonable and ran *away* in an effort to escape the storm. However, the wise Shepherd knew the course of the storm and called for them to stop. He sent the sheep that had heard His command down a slight ravine where a perfect shelter was awaiting them under a rocky ledge. Once again, it had proven beneficial to stay close enough to the Shepherd to hear His voice.

Since some of the sheep had already gone too far to hear Him, He left in search of them. The noise and wind were alarming as the storm hovered over the sheltered sheep, and they shook with fear for those who had not made it inside. Finally, several sheep came stumbling in, but the Shepherd was not with them. When He did return, undaunted by the fierce storm, He was carrying three trembling lambs that had simply followed the older sheep in the wrong direction. How important it is for the mature sheep to listen to the Shepherd's voice and follow Him. Thankfully, He is merciful.

Although children do not always behave accordingly, they really do desire an example to follow. As parents, we are the most natural choice—God planned it that way. No person, place, or thing is worth risking the loss of our children. When a parent goes down a wrong path, it results in heart-wrenching upheaval in the home and always leaves the children vulnerable to a vast assortment of storms. Many times the parents find their way back, but the children may be lost until our merciful God is able to seek them out and carry them back to safety.

Children trust their parents to respond correctly to life's storms, and they follow them. When we face a storm of temptation, disappointment, or fear, it is wise to remember those we are leading before we respond to the storm. The familiar Proverbs 22:6 states, "Train a child in the way he should go, and when he is old he will not turn from it" (NIV). We take an active role in training our children on a daily basis. From the basic tasks of shoe-tying and bed-making to significant choices of right and wrong, we are *actively* instructing and guiding our children.

However, often without realizing it, we are *passively* training them in an even greater way through our actions. This happens in a negative way when we neglect our own parents or keep extra change from the sales clerk. We may call our workplace and say we are sick when we are really well, or we may direct our children to "tell the caller I'm not home." Or we instruct our children, "Do as I say, not as I do." We are training our children all the time, and they are taking notes!

We need the Shepherd's wisdom and guidance to parent young lives, even without a storm. And when the storms do come, staying close to Him and listening to the direction of His Word will secure a safe haven to ride out the storm—safe for us and for our children.

Chapter 18

THE ROCKSLIDE

THE ACTIONS OF OTHERS, INTENTIONAL OR HAPHAZARD, affect our lives every day. For example, a simple action such as changing lanes in busy traffic may start a chain reaction through a car accident that affects the lives of dozens of unsuspecting individuals. However, this does not bring fear to the heart of those who follow God and believe that "All things work together for *good* to those who love God and are called according to His purpose" (Rom. 8:28, NKJV, emphasis added).

A lone sheep standing on a ledge on the face of a rocky mountain desperately wanted to join the flock that was grazing on a higher plateau. The path up the mountain was visible to this point, but there was no path to continue on to the plateau. The sheep looked frustrated and bewildered. Where should it go? Should it return down the mountain or just stay here?

Just then, a slight rumble on the mountainside preceded a tumultuous rockslide that cascaded to the side of the ledge. The solitary sheep turned its head from the dusty spray. However, when the dust had settled, it discovered a conspicuous ledge that continued from the point where it stood and was wide enough to lead it up and around the mountain face to the plateau. A grazing sheep on the plateau above never realized that its movements had caused a liberating rockslide for the sheep stranded below.

Hermits cloister themselves in solitary confinement to avoid interaction with others. The causes are many—betrayal, abandonment, or simply a compulsion to resist interference. This is an unnatural attitude toward life because we were created to be in relationship with others. We travel through life in groups, just like sheep.

However, solitude possesses a certain appeal as an alternative to negative experiences we suffer because of another's action. Whether it is a car accident, a stolen purse, or a flu epidemic, our response is to cry out, "Where's the *good* in this? Life is already a struggle. Where in God's *purpose* for me does this fit?" The inconvenience of car repairs and doctor visits, credit card replacements, missed work, or concerns for our ill child only add grief to the challenges and frustrations we are already facing. We are already bewildered standing on that lonely ledge. Why do we need a rockslide?

When Jesus was here on earth, the lives of His disciples were, at the very least, challenging. Because of their belief that He was the Messiah, they left their professions, traveled from town to town at His will, and met with great opposition from religious leaders. Just when they were beginning to understand and accept this man and His lifestyle, He was arrested and crucified.

Talk about a rockslide! Yes, they scattered in shock and in fear for their lives, but they soon realized that the rockslide—the crucifixion—provided the way for all mankind to receive eternal life. Armed with this knowledge, they took the gospel and, as it was said of them "turned the world upside down" (Acts 17:6, KJV). They started a chain reaction that affects our lives today and is fulfilling His purposes.

If we truly believe that ALL things—not just the happy, feel-good things—work together for our good, our cry will be in cadence with David's victorious song of Psalm 56:3–4, "When I am afraid, I will put my trust in you. I praise God for what he has promised. I trust in God, so why should I be afraid? What can *mere mortals* do to me?" (emphasis added).

Catastrophic rockslides become opportunities for us to move on from frustrating circumstances and be liberated from bewildering situations. We do not comprehend how God uses our negative experiences to bring about positive results, but we know that He can take the painful blunders or ill intentions of one individual and turn them into something good in the life of another. He is faithful to fulfill His purposes.

Chapter 19

PURPOSEFUL RESTRAINT

ALTHOUGH IT IS REASSURING WHEN RESTRAINT IS applied to a vicious animal or human, it is rarely comfortable when we are restrained. The weight and strength of a toddler in its mother's arms is greatly magnified when it desires to roam rather than to be restrained. The behavior of a prisoner in his confinement is a true test of character. From the very young to the mature, no one enjoys restraint.

However, we will have occasions in our lives when God holds us closer and tighter than we desire so that He might fulfill His purpose.

As the Shepherd led the flock on an extensive journey, two lambs scampered about at His feet, enjoying their liberty. He held a third lamb tightly in His arms, and at first, it wiggled in protest. Eventually, however, it accepted the Shepherd's restraint and absorbed the scenery from its vantage point close to His heart. When the Shepherd paused for a short rest on the rolling terrain, the two lambs on the ground saw only the next hilly mound ahead of them, but the carried lamb viewed a much different picture from its lofty position. Just over the next hill it spied a flowering meadow and a sparkling lake, a promise of certain refreshment.

Later in the day when the two lambs were tired from their journey and somewhat discouraged, the Shepherd released the lamb He had carried. Filled with excitement of the promises it knew lay just ahead, it ran, coaxing and encouraging the others to finish the journey. Their hope was renewed.

God uses an unlimited number of methods to instruct us along the path of life. Although we are content and pleased just to follow Him, He, more often than not, is planning something of a more eternal nature for us. He will hold us in a position or a place that is uncomfortable or challenging, tightening His grip until we accept His restraint. He will test our trust in His leadership and our willingness to submit to it. This is where the *eternal* aspect begins—lessons learned, promises revealed, and hopes renewed.

The story of Joseph is one of the most compelling biblical illustrations of character testing. (See Genesis 37–46.) Introduced to us as a proud, boastful, yet favored young boy, Joseph was sold into slavery by his brothers and later wrongfully imprisoned in Egypt. Psalm 105:17–19 explains that in God's dealings with Israel, "He sent someone to Egypt ahead of them—Joseph, who was sold as a slave. They bruised his feet with fetters and placed his neck in an iron collar. Until the time came to fulfill His dreams, the LORD tested Joseph's character."

We do not know all that Joseph experienced during the restraints of his slavery and prison confinement, but we do know that he trusted God's leadership in his life and submitted to it. Humility and integrity replaced the negative characteristics in his life; and through the interpretation of dreams and visions, he became the tool that God used to save the nations of Egypt and Israel from famine. Hope was renewed.

If we are stuck in a dead-end job or lying in a hospital bed, we may become the answer to a mother's prayer for the salvation of a son or daughter who occupies the space next to us. When we stop lamenting God's restraint and start absorbing the scenery, we can see that He has an eternal purpose. As we have learned from the writings of the Apostle Paul, prison bars cannot prevent the human spirit from touching eternity. Even from the confinement of a wheelchair, many have touched the world for eternity with their songs, written word, and art.

Unlike the little lamb and Joseph, we can choose to resist the purpose of the Shepherd's restraint. Eventually the confinement may pass, but more than likely we will encounter it again in the future. It has been said that because of God's great mercy, we never really fail His tests. We just take them over and over until we pass.

Chapter 20

GREENER PASTURES

WHEN GOD HOLDS US IN A PLACE WHERE WE DO NOT want to be, we do everything we can to break free. The appeal of freedom draws us away from the place He has chosen for us. Most of the time, He simply holds us tighter—but occasionally He just lets us go.

A young sheep was struggling to get out of the Shepherd's arms, pushing and jabbing with its legs. Most of the bystanders understood this behavior for they, too, had at one time or another desired a different landscape, greener pastures. After a while, the Shepherd just let the lamb go, and it fell to the ground, its legs sprawled out in all directions. The impact was more shocking than it was painful.

Slowly, the young sheep pushed itself up and started nudging the Shepherd in an effort to receive His attention. It did not realize that freedom would cause physical pain, not to mention the sting of being ignored by the Shepherd. The wise Shepherd was not really rejecting the sheep, but rather waiting for it to *desire* the place He had chosen for it. After a while, the Shepherd bent down and picked up the hurting animal. It completely relaxed in His arms as He moved on His way with many sheep following.

We all face occasions when we look over the fence at greener pastures or become discontent where we are in a relationship, a job, our stewardship, or even a ministry. When we struggle for freedom to pursue our desires, we often find ourselves even more deeply entrenched in dissatisfaction for a longer period of time. However, sometimes God just lets us go, and we suffer pain that is greater than the lack of freedom—loneliness, unemployment, bankruptcy. At such times, we must swallow our pride, ask forgiveness for being resistant to His will, and return to the place He has chosen for us.

Jonah, the reluctant Old Testament prophet, refused God's place for him and went seeking for greener pastures. When God let him go, he called out from the belly of a fish, "When I had lost all hope, I turned my thoughts once more to the Lord. And my earnest prayer went out to you" (Jon. 2:7, TLB). Verse 10 records that "then the Lord ordered the fish to spit up Jonah on the beach and it did." After three days of isolation and distress inside the fish, Jonah viewed Nineveh as a very desirable place; and God gave him fruitful ministry there.

Hopefully, when we return to His arms—His appointed place for us—we will have learned to accept without resistance *all* the places He has chosen for us. In His arms, we are certain to hear His voice; when we stop struggling, we are able to listen to what He is saying.

Chapter 21
RECEIVING DISCIPLINE

DISCIPLINE IS PAINFUL. IT IS MEANT TO BE. WHETHER IT is disciplining the body for a great race or receiving the Lord's discipline for life's journey, there is a measure of pain. Our response to discipline usually determines its length and intensity.

Even while the flock followed the Shepherd, it faced many dangers along the path. A ram slipped away from the Shepherd's care and entered the path of an approaching snake. The Shepherd, always aware of His sheep's whereabouts, briskly plucked him from the impending danger. The shaken ram longed to be cradled and assured that all was well, but instead the Shepherd tied him on a very short rope that kept him close to His side and returned in silence to the flock.

After wallowing in self-pity for a considerable length of time, the ram finally accepted his fate. After all, he left the security of the Shepherd in disobedience and put himself in harm's way. Perhaps the ram recalled the Shepherd's character throughout the long journey and realized the restriction was not imposed to prevent his freedom, but to promote his safety. He was loved.

At the moment of the sheep's revelation, the Shepherd casually reached down to pet him. It was as if He knew that the sheep was accepting His discipline at that precise time. And, of course, He did know.

Whether our discipline is in the form of restrictions, separation, actual pain, or other means, our submission to it will better equip us for life's journey. Self-pity is debilitating and only serves to focus on the pain instead of the lesson to be learned and the greater truth that God loves us. Hebrews 12:5–7, 11, reminds us, "My child, don't *make light of* the LORD's discipline, and don't *give up* when he corrects you. For the LORD disciplines those he *loves,* and he punishes each one he accepts as His child.... No discipline is enjoyable while it is happening—it's painful! But afterward there will be a peaceful harvest of *right* living for those who are trained in this way" (emphasis added).

When we are receiving discipline from the Lord, we should follow the example of the sheep *after* he stopped wallowing in self-pity. We will shorten the length and lessen the intensity of our discipline by examining our situation honestly and remembering the character of the Shepherd in times past. As we accept our discipline and learn from it, we will realize that He loves us.

Read the psalmist's testimony of a lesson learned, "I used to wander off until you disciplined me; but now I closely follow your word" (Ps. 119:67).

Chapter 22

MUD IN YOUR EYE

WE NEVER KNOW WHAT A DAY WILL BRING TO US. WE can be faithfully following the Shepherd, at peace with the world, and in a split second we can have our legs knocked out from under us and find ourselves face down in the mud. Where's the justice in that? Well, life is tough, but God is faithful.

Dark, heavy clouds hung over the flock as the Shepherd led the sheep down a muddy slope in the pouring rain. The wool of the sheep became saturated, making it extremely difficult for them to move. This was a trying situation at best; but to make matters worse, a mudslide enveloped several of the sheep, carried them twenty feet down the slope, and buried them.

The Shepherd guided the greater part of the flock back to the fold and quickly returned to the mudslide. Wading through the mud, He found them, one by one, and pulled each one to solid ground. He carefully cleared the mud from their faces, and soon life began to return to their limp bodies. Then He removed the thick mud from their limbs, enabling them to walk, and led them back to the fold.

As the returning sheep entered the fold with their Shepherd, the sheep that were already there stirred with excitement. The Shepherd had brought deliverance when things looked so bleak. No wonder they followed Him!

It can be rough in the trenches. In fact, the story goes, weary soldiers coined the phrase, "Here's mud in your eye!" as they toasted to good health and safety in the trenches of World War I. The temporary spray of blinding mud was better than the full impact of the artillery that caused the spray. But regardless of our good wishes, we learn at a fairly young age that bad things can happen to good people. A single phone call, a simple action, or a thoughtless word can send us on a downward spiral of despair no matter how closely we follow the Shepherd. At moments like these, we seldom recall the thousands of sorrows we have been spared in life. It's as if mud gets in our eyes, and we temporarily lose sight of our Shepherd and His power to deliver us.

When Jesus and His disciples encountered a blind man in John 9, His disciples asked Him whose sin caused this blindness. Jesus assured them that no one's sin had caused it, but that God's power would be seen through the healing of the man. Then He proceeded to put mud over the eyes of the blind man, and when the mud was washed away, the man could see! He discovered that the Lord, who created the earth, can use any part of it to exhibit His power. Mud and the tough things that life throws our way are opportunities for God to display His greatness.

What a reassurance it is when Jesus opens our eyes, and we realize that we follow a God who is right there with us in the trenches! He is faithful to deliver us, set us back on solid ground, clear away our heartaches, and walk us back to wholeness. No one understood this better than David when he wrote:

> I waited patiently for the Lord to help me, and he turned to me and heard my cry. He lifted me out of the pit of despair, out of the *mud* and *mire*. He set my feet on solid ground and steadied me as I walked along. He has given me a *new song* to sing, a hymn of praise to our God. Many will see what he has done and be amazed. They will put their trust in the Lord.
>
> —Psalm 40:1–3, emphasis added

Our difficult experiences enable us to understand the despair that others sometimes feel, and we are able to offer them the hope of deliverance. The testimony of our own deliverance will cause others to put their trust in God. Life is tough, but God is faithful.

So, here's mud in your eye!

Chapter 23

WAITING FOR THE BEST

PATIENCE IS ONE OF LIFE'S GREAT VIRTUES. HOWEVER, living in our "instant" culture does not help to develop this virtue in us. We have instant oatmeal, pre-fab housing, digital photos, online banking, express mail, fast food, and an Internet that puts the world at our fingertips. We sit in front of a huge wide screen and watch experts solve all of life's problems in two hours. And because patience is a virtue to be desired, we cry, "Lord, give me patience and hurry up about it."

Peering over the cliff, the Shepherd and a ewe from the flock looked out over the countryside for a suitable place to graze. It all appeared the same to the ewe; and although she patiently waited, she could not understand the delay.

The Shepherd's discerning eye was looking for the most beneficial place—the best place for His flock. This is what distinguished Him from other shepherds. Soon He saw an area somewhat hidden by the terrain where just a small corner of dark green was exposed. The Shepherd knew that the dark foliage not only meant rich grazing land, but also refreshing water. The good Shepherd always provides what is best for the flock just when they need it the most.

The most incredible aspect of this scenario is that the ewe waited *patiently*. Because we are impatient by nature, we find it difficult to wait for God's timing; however, whether it is finding a pair of shoes, a fulfilling job, or a mate for life, the Good Shepherd knows the right fit. The shepherds of fate, chance, convenience, or the biological clock will never care enough to provide the very best for us when we need it the most.

Genesis 29–31, the account of the Old Testament patriarch, Jacob, and his challenge of securing a wife, reveals a man of exemplary patience. It tells how Jacob, after finding Rachel—the love of his life—was tricked by his father-in-law into first marrying his love's older sister of questionable beauty. In keeping with the custom of the day, Jacob eventually labored a total of fourteen years to fulfill a seven-year agreement for the hand of Rachel in marriage.

Although Jacob certainly must have questioned God's timing, he patiently waited for God to act, all the while producing a very large family. Finally, the Lord spoke to Jacob in Genesis 31:3, "Return to the land of your father and grandfather and to your relatives there, and I will be with you." Jacob left with great wealth and the beginning of a great nation.

God always provides what is best for us, when we need it the most. Imagine walking through a doorway with nothing on the other side—a freefall is certain. He never opens a door until there is a place to enter. If we find ourselves standing on a precipice with God looking out over our future with anticipation, let us follow the advice of David, a man who spent a great deal of his life waiting. He encouraged us, "Wait patiently for the LORD. Be brave and courageous. Yes, wait patiently for the LORD" (Ps. 27:14). Our Shepherd knows best.

Chapter 24

THE LADDER OF SUCCESS

WE TEND TO MEASURE SUCCESS BY THE STATUS WE have achieved and the possessions we have accumulated. However, it should come as no surprise to those who follow the Lord that He evaluates success by a completely different standard.

One of the Shepherd's many responsibilities is to secure rich grazing land for the sheep. When such land is not easily visible, He will go to great lengths to find it, and this is what He did one particular day. He called to the sheep to stay as He ventured out on a dangerous ledge, peering through the cliffs to the valley below.

A ram in the flock was eager to show his bravery and commitment to the Shepherd, and ignoring the command to stay, followed Him. The ledge required greater dexterity than the ram possessed, and within moments he fell into a precarious position on the ledge below. In response to the bleating sheep's cry for help, the Shepherd stopped looking for food and came to find him. He gently coaxed him to a place of safety and then resumed His search for grazing land. The shaken sheep returned to the flock, having shown only that he failed to obey.

The brave ram was not successful in his venture to prove his commitment to the Shepherd. His heart appeared to be right, but heroics, no matter how well intentioned, can reveal a lack of maturity. An action that appears to be a huge step of faith and a willingness to be martyred may be nothing more than simple disobedience. Just like the sheep, we may sincerely desire to do great exploits for God and show our commitment to Him; however, just as the Shepherd desired of the sheep, He first wants our obedience. Whether He says stay or go, eat or fast, kill or spare, our success before Him is determined by our obedience to what He has said.

In 1 Samuel 15, God commanded King Saul to destroy everything in the nation of Amalek because of their opposition to Israel. Saul chose to destroy only those things that were worthless and spared the best of the sheep and cattle to be used in sacrifice to God. In and of itself, this act appeared to be worthy, but in light of God's command to destroy *everything,* Saul was disobedient. He erected a monument to himself and was intending to offer a sacrifice to God when the prophet Samuel confronted him and asked, "What is more pleasing to the LORD: your burnt offerings and sacrifices or your obedience to his voice? Listen! *Obedience is better than sacrifice*" (1 Sam. 15:22, emphasis added). Within days, Samuel anointed a new king—Saul was unsuccessful.

God is not against the sacrifices we make for Him, but He does reject the sacrifices we make instead of obedience. We may be a workaholic in our careers or our churches, yet be completely disobedient to His will for us. Our homes may have an open door to any who comes, yet lack the order and peace that God desires for them; they may be a decorator's dream, but harbor no love. Position and wealth are often blessings that come because of obedience, but they can also be achieved through our sacrifices *instead* of our obedience. God views all these things through His "obedience filter," and He determines our success.

Our obedience may be viewed as a ladder of success reaching to the heavens. Each act of obedience brings us one rung closer to Him, one step closer to hearing His words, "Well done, my good and faithful servant" (Matt. 25:21). This the way God evaluates success.

Chapter 25

The Protective Cloak

Photo credit: Barbara Cassell

THE ELITE ARE A SEGMENT OF OUR SOCIETY THAT considers itself a cut above others, more intelligent than most. They are especially superior to the dumb sheep that must follow a shepherd. The elite are everywhere—in the media, in Hollywood, in our universities, and in our neighborhoods. They accuse those who follow God of being weak, mindless, and indecisive. But their words cannot harm those who take refuge under the Shepherd's protective cloak.

A tremendous storm was brewing over the grazing flock. The Shepherd, ever mindful of the weather, stretched out His cloak, called His sheep, and gathered them in under its safety. As torrents of rain, lightening, and debris fell all around the huddled group, the sheep were safe under His seemingly endless cloak of protection.

After the storm had ended, the sheep walked out from under their covering to find a sobering landscape. Several sheep were lying on the ground. They moved around them, nudged them, did whatever they could to raise them, but to no avail. It appeared that these lifeless sheep were so focused on the storm that they failed to get under the protective cloak. With great sadness, the surviving sheep walked away and moved on.

How unfortunate that some of the sheep could not get their focus off the storm to see the protection the Shepherd was offering and hear His call! Perhaps the flashes of lightning mesmerized them, or possibly they had the attitude that they were not going to take this assault lying down. Some may have denied the storm's ferocity and decided to stick it out. Regardless of the reason, they died because they did not have the good sense to listen to the Shepherd and get out of the rain.

The storm with its rain, lightening, and debris is symbolic of the assault of insults, slander, and false accusations that the elite direct toward those who follow after God. However, the storm did not injure the sheep that ran to the Shepherd's safe covering. David, a shepherd who certainly understood the weather, described God's protection for us in Psalm 31:20, "You hide them in the shelter of your presence, safe from those who conspire against them. You shelter them in your presence far from accusing tongues." David was a brave warrior, yet he knew when to run for cover. He himself cried, "I look to you for protection. I will hide beneath the shadow of your wings until the danger passes by" (Ps. 57:1).

When our adversaries accuse us of being weak because we follow God, our best response to the storm is to share truth and pray for God to change the hearts of the accusers. Even though it is difficult to do in the heat of a confrontation, we must practice the valuable instruction Paul gave to young Timothy:

> Again I say, don't get involved in foolish, ignorant arguments that only start fights. A servant of the Lord must not quarrel but must be kind to everyone, be able to teach, and be patient with difficult people. Gently instruct those who oppose the truth. *Perhaps God will change those people's hearts, and they will learn the truth.*
>
> —2 Timothy 2:23–25, emphasis added

Our antagonistic neighbors, critical business partners, and radical teachers may never know what hit them when God acts in response to our prayers and touches their lives. And while we are on our knees praying for them, we would do well to remember those who experience more than insults because of their faith. Around the world many also endure great physical suffering and death. Under the covering of the Shepherd, their spirits will never fall to the enemy.

As with David and Paul, the surviving sheep refused to submit to the personal storm directed against them and were able to move on to new challenges and victories. When we do the same, we are able to continue on as God's response to a much greater attack than mere name-calling, and that is the rising tide of secularism that desires to remove God from our holidays, currency, education, and ultimately our lives. We can stop this tide by placing in positions of government, through our vote, those who will respect and protect our beliefs and also by standing firmly with and supporting those whom God has placed on the frontlines to expose this enemy.

As we war against this true enemy of our faith, and accusations and insults are hurled at us because of it, we can run to His presence for protection and tell Him all about the injustice of our accusers. While the Lord invites us to open our hearts to Him, He has answered the deepest heart concerns. In Matthew 5:11–12, He said:

> God blesses you when people mock you and persecute and lie about you…because you are my followers. Be happy about it! Be very glad! For a great reward awaits you in heaven.

Chapter 26

UNREASONABLE PEACE

As long as we follow the Shepherd, we can be certain that His enemy is also our enemy. The fact that this is true—that we have an enemy—accomplishes one favorable result. We are certain to stay close to the Shepherd when we hear the lions roaring and the wolves howling.

The Shepherd and the flock were in a terrible spot! A large pack of wolves had surrounded them as they rested and grazed on the shady hillside. The sheep closed in around the Shepherd as He spoke to them, but they were unable to hear Him because of the deafening howls of the wolves.

In spite of this predicament, the sheep were at peace, content and unafraid. It appeared so strange, but a closer examination of the situation brought understanding. Even though they could not hear all the comforting words of the Shepherd, the sheep had fixed their eyes on His face. His calm expression and His eyes of love spoke volumes to them, and they were at peace.

Just before Jewish leaders picked up stones to kill him, Stephen, an early church leader, saw a vision of the Lord Himself. Acts 7:59–60 concludes the story, "And as they stoned him, Stephen *prayed*, 'Lord Jesus, receive my spirit.' He fell to his knees, shouting, 'Lord, don't charge them with this sin!' And with that, he died" (emphasis added). New Testament missionaries Paul and Silas were severely beaten and thrown into prison, and Acts 16:25 records, "Around midnight Paul and Silas were praying and singing hymns to God."

These are just two examples of the unreasonable peace God's people—Joshua, Gideon, David, Daniel, and so many others—have experienced in the midst of trouble when they fixed their eyes on the Lord. It is a peace we can have when there is no earthly reason to have it, a phenomenon Paul described when he wrote, "And the peace of God, which *transcends all understanding,* will guard your hearts and your minds in Christ Jesus." (Phil. 4:7, NIV, emphasis added).

When our enemy is howling at us, we, too, must fix our eyes on the Shepherd's face if we want to receive this peace. But how do we see His face? We see His eyes of love through the written Word—a portrait of His everlasting love for us. We see the wise, caring expression on His face when we look in the mirror—a reflection or record of all He has done to personally guide us. Remembering His faithfulness brings peace and contentment, and we are not afraid. When we focus intently on Him, we no longer hear the howls and roars of the enemy; in fact, we may not even be aware that they exist.

Such is the nature of the Shepherd's unreasonable peace. An old chorus communicates it so well: "Turn your eyes upon Jesus. Look full in His wonderful face, and the things of earth will grow strangely dim, in the light of His glory and grace."[1]

Chapter 21

PROCEED WITH CAUTION

GOD LOVES TO BLESS HIS CHILDREN WITH UPGRADES—newly opened doors, more comfortable lifestyles, and greater realms of influence. As He reveals Himself to us in this way, we adapt quite quickly to our new surroundings and yearn to explore all the advantages they afford. In our excitement, however, we must proceed with caution.

The Shepherd picked up a lamb that needed extra attention and raised it to His shoulder as he cuddled and stroked it. From this vantage point, the scenery was so different for the lamb. In fact, it was a whole new world.

As the Shepherd walked amongst the trees, the lamb stretched its neck as far as it could to reach out and nibble on the lower branches. However, the special treat from the Shepherd ended abruptly when He pulled the yearning lamb away from the branch and gently spoke, "No, this would not be good for you." The innocent lamb did not see what the Shepherd saw—a snake poised in the branches, ready to strike.

When a blessing comes our way, we want to wallow in it, milk it for all it's worth, and leave no stone unturned, all the while we are reaching for the stars. It may be wise, however, to proceed with caution on this virgin turf and heed the warnings of the One who brought us to this lofty height. Even the beloved David was swayed by apparent favor, "When I was prosperous I said, 'Nothing can stop me now!' Your favor, O LORD, made me as secure as a mountain. Then you turned away from me, and I was shattered" (Ps. 30:6–7).

A job promotion, a hefty raise, or new influential friends may introduce us to situations and temptations that we, in our innocence, never knew existed. Our promotion may lead us to a luncheon table where deals are signed and sealed with one drink, and then another, and another. Our newfound wealth may allow us to acquire many, many things we do not need.

We may be exposed to things that could actually bring harm to our homes and activities that could have a negative effect on us even though they may be acceptable to our new friends. The Lord may find it necessary to pull us away from some of the attractive things that we greatly desire because He knows they would not be good for us.

Pride is often the first danger that is poised and ready to strike. The account of the Judean king Hezekiah in 2 Kings 18–20 delivers a cautionary message for us. Hezekiah was a good man whose personal relationship with God helped him to change the political and religious atmosphere of Judah for the better. God blessed him with great wealth and a miraculous physical healing.

Unfortunately, somewhere along the line, Hezekiah became proud of what he had achieved and arrogantly displayed all his wealth to visiting dignitaries from the distant country of Babylon. While this may have seemed harmless at the time, the memory of it may well have been the catalyst that caused the future mighty Babylonian army to conquer Judah and carry off its wealth as prophesied by Isaiah in 2 Kings 20:16–18. The life of Hezekiah serves as an incentive to give honor to God for all His goodness and not to solicit honor for ours.

The Lord desires that we have a growing maturity that responds to blessings with the heart of the psalmist in Psalm 119:65–68 (emphasis added):

> You have done many *good things* for me, LORD, just as you promised. I believe in your commands; now teach me *good judgment* and knowledge. I used to wander off until you disciplined me; but now I closely follow your

word. You are good and do only good; teach me your decrees.

Additional blessings are sure to follow when we proceed with caution.

Chapter 28

Our Safest Position

All who live in a prosperous nation may find themselves surrounded by too much of a good thing. There is too much food, too much clothing, too much paperwork, too much technology, too much information—just too much stuff that requires too much attention! It all requires vigilance to stay close to the Shepherd.

Grazing on a windy hill under the Shepherd's watchful eye, a lamb enjoyed the abundance of flowering herbs. The lamb was so completely enthralled with the fragrance and taste of its delightful feast that it unwittingly wandered away from the Shepherd. As it moved close to the edge of the hilltop, a strong wind came and carried it to the ground below.

The lamb cried for help as the earth rose to meet it. However, to its amazement, the Shepherd was already there, opening wide His soft, billowing garment to catch it. A forceful bounce on the cloth produced a momentary loss of breath, but the lamb was saved.

Frightened nearly to death by this unplanned adventure, the lamb stayed close to the Shepherd's side, and they walked together for quite some time. After a while, the wise Shepherd encouraged the lamb, "It's all right to enjoy the flowers, but always in sight of where I am."

It is remarkable that the Shepherd, knowing our nature as He does, continues to provide so many wonderful blessings for us. If we agree with David that "He fills my life with good things" (Ps. 103:5), then we may assume that He is the ultimate source of our bountiful tables, bulging closets, limitless Internet, and wide-screened televisions, and abundant flowering herbs. Like the lamb, we may find it difficult to know just when to stop pursuing these blessings before we wander into a place of danger.

As the Shepherd's faithful followers, it is rare for us to

intentionally become obsessive about all the good things in our lives. Unfortunately, our "stuff" requires so much attention. We purchase trendy clothes through as many as a dozen catalogs we receive through the mail, and we must provide the proper care and cleaning for them. This is especially true when we spill food on them from the gastronomical meal we prepared after viewing the food channel on our high definition television. At the end of the day, completely exhausted from our multitude of errands, we fall into bed where we must decide the most comfortable number on which to sleep.

Before we unknowingly move too close to the edge of our hilltop by pursuing the *next* good thing, it is prudent for us to examine our position ahead of a prevailing wind that could send us aloft. We must be careful that our pursuits do not resemble the Apostle Paul's description, "For a greedy person is really an idolater, worshiping the things of this world" (Eph. 5:5). We must not allow ourselves to be so enthralled with the fragrance and taste of our pursuits that we lose sight of the Shepherd and become like those who "worshiped and served created things rather than the Creator—who is forever praised" (Rom. 1:25, NIV).

When we pray for God's blessings and enlarged territory, as Jabez did in 1 Chronicles 4:9, we must also pray that we will have a greater desire for His *presence* than we have ever known. Our safest position is to be close to the Shepherd, where we can hear His voice. Thankfully, the Shepherd watches over our interaction with the blessings He has provided. Even though the lamb lost sight of the Shepherd, He never lost sight of the lamb.

Our Shepherd knows exactly what we need even before we

ask Him (see Matthew 6:8), and He "hears his people when they call to him for help [and] he rescues them from all their troubles" (Ps. 34:17). As a result, He was there to rescue the lamb from its terrifying fall. Because the lamb was fearful about leaving the Shepherd's side after this, He encouraged it to enjoy the good things He had created, but always with reverence to Him. Psalm 95:6–7 exhorts us:

> Come, let us worship and bow down. Let us kneel before the LORD our maker, for he is our God. We are the people he watches over, the flock under his care.

We worship our Shepherd, and He watches over us. We can never have too much of *this* good thing.

Chapter 29

THE SHEPHERD'S DELIGHT

WHEN WE EXPERIENCE DIFFICULT TIMES, IT SEEMS VERY unnatural to give praise and thanksgiving to the Lord. It feels more natural, more comfortable, to whine and complain to Him or even withdraw from Him. Yet, if we honor God with our praise and our trust when it seems unnatural, we find the greatest peace and contentment.

Sitting on the shore of a great lake, the Shepherd cooled His feet in the water and refreshed Himself. This was where He went for pleasure, a place that seemed unnatural for the sheep. Many sheep wanted to be close to the Shepherd, but as the waves rolled in, they would back away from them in fear. One sheep, however, desperately wanted to stay where the Shepherd laughed with joy, and it remained with Him. Trembling, the sheep caught hold of the Shepherd's coat with its teeth and held on tightly under the force of the pelting waves.

The Shepherd covered the sheep with His garments as He picked it up and embraced it. In that secure place, all apprehension left the sheep, and the most incredible peace and contentment overwhelmed it. As it followed the Shepherd and did the unnatural, it was blessed.

When we go through difficult times, a logical way to find the comfort and peace of the Lord is to go where we know He will be—a place that delights and gives pleasure to Him. Psalm 147:11 promises, "The LORD's delight is in those who fear him, those who put their hope in his unfailing love." When we honor Him with thanksgiving and praise, despite our circumstances, He takes pleasure in it. God declared in Psalm 50:23, "Giving thanks is a sacrifice that truly honors me."

Sometimes our difficulties are so overwhelming that we have to remind ourselves to praise Him. David understood this when he wrote Psalm 103:1, "Praise the Lord, *I tell myself*; with my whole heart, I will praise His holy name.

Praise the Lord, *I tell myself,* and never forget the good things He does for me" (emphasis added). Over the next several psalms, David followed his self-directed exhortation with a long list of blessings for which to praise Him. He concluded in Psalm 107:43 with the declaration, "Those who are wise will take all this to heart; they will see in our history the faithful love of the LORD."

The Lord also takes pleasure in the details of our lives. In the words of Psalm 37:23, "The LORD directs the steps of the godly. He *delights* in every detail" (emphasis added). Most often, it is the many details of life that cause us the greatest difficulty, pelting us one after the other. It is only natural to back away from them. Yet, just as the trembling sheep had the right idea when it latched onto the Shepherd, it is wise for us to cling to the One who actually takes pleasure in the details of our difficult times.

When the details and difficulties of life surround us, we must do the unnatural thing. We must run to the Lord with thanksgiving and praise on our lips, cling tenaciously to Him, and be overwhelmed by the peace and the contentment of His presence.

Chapter 30

Unlimited Resources

Some of the many great benefits of following the Shepherd are the unlimited resources He has made available to us. In Psalm 50:10–12, God declares:

> For all the animals of the forest are mine, and I own the cattle on a thousand hills. I know every bird of the mountains, and all the animals of the field are mine. If

I were hungry, I would not tell you, for all the world is mine and everything in it.

The Shepherd and His flock had been traveling for many days, and they were hot, tired, and thirsty. When the Shepherd came to a well, He started pouring water in a circular trough that surrounded the well. As the refreshing water diminished, He poured more out into the trough. The sheep did not push or shove. They knew from experience that there would always be enough water when the Shepherd was providing, and they were grateful.

When the Shepherd poured water into the trough that encircled the well, He illustrated His circle of provision that is without beginning or end. Similarly, all of nature enjoys a circle or cycle of living. Although God must certainly appreciate our efforts as His gardeners to protect and conserve His earth, it must amuse Him when we think that anything we do during our brief stint on earth could save the planet. As the earth cycles through warm and cool stages, God controls not only these temperatures, but also recruits the weather to prune and change the earth's landscaping.

God's resources are not limited to what *we* have already discovered. In his search for wisdom, Solomon wrote in Ecclesiastes 8:17, "No one can discover everything God is doing under the sun. Not even the wisest people discover everything, no matter what they claim." Only God knows the bounty yet to be revealed. Through the promise of His word, we know that "He satisfies the thirsty and fills the hungry with good things" (Ps. 107:9).

There was no pushing or shoving around the trough because the sheep trusted the Shepherd's unlimited resources. Because the trough had limited space for the vast flock to quench its thirst, it was required that the satisfied sheep move aside for others to drink. The circle of provision was successful as long as the sheep were not greedy. So it is with God's provision for us. We reveal our gratitude and appreciation to our Provider by the thoughtful use of our vast natural resources. Instead of consuming them greedily, we are to cultivate them. "Remember this—a farmer who plants only a few seeds will get a small crop. But the one who plants generously will get a generous crop" (2 Cor. 9:6).

Equally important is the fact that a grateful heart moves so others can enjoy God's provision. Because of the mistakes or greed of others, millions of hungry people find it difficult to understand the concept of God's unlimited resources. Yet, He has provided for them—through us. When their tremendous need touches our grateful hearts, we are *moved* to satisfy their hunger. Paul encouraged us in 2 Corinthians 9:9–11:

> As the scriptures say, "They share freely and give generously to the poor. Their good deeds will be remembered forever." For God is the one who provides seed for the farmer and then bread to eat. In the same way, he will provide and increase your resources, and then produce a great harvest of generosity in you. Yes, you will be enriched in every way so that you can always be generous. And when we take your gifts to those who need them, they will thank God.

God provides everything we need through His unlimited resources. We are satisfied, we *move,* others are satisfied, and all are thankful to God. It is a circle of provision without beginning or end.

Chapter 31

Rest Assured

WHEN GOD FORMED US FROM THE DUST OF THE EARTH, He could have put us in bodies of steel, created us as hard as diamonds, or molded us out of Styrofoam. Instead, He chose to give us physical, flesh-and-blood houses that require rest and relaxation. We often neglect this need for rest because we keep going, doing, and being in an effort to meet the many demands of life. Just like the energizer bunny—we keep going and going and going.

One day the Shepherd led the flock to a grassy hillside and stretched out on the silky grass to rest. An energetic young sheep ran up to the Shepherd, jumping and prancing all around Him, trying desperately to awaken Him.

After expending all its energy in its unproductive attempt to move the Shepherd, the weary, frustrated sheep finally nestled up against Him and rested. An amazing peace came to that serene hillside and the resting flock that lay there.

We all know people who are not equipped with a "stop" button. For these people, something is always moving—whether it is the mouth talking, the foot tapping, the fingers snapping, or the mind clicking. Events of one kind or another are always happening. They are exciting—and exhausting—to be around.

How do these people harness so much energy and why do they deserve it? For many, it is simply genetics; a parent or grandparent may have possessed this attribute. Others may gain increased vigor from too many stimulants—coffee, sugar, chocolate. Still others are completely moved by the massive need for order, cleanliness, happiness, or just plain good deeds. Feelings of guilt plague some who believe that lack of productivity is a sin. They forget that even God took a day off to rest and to enjoy what He had created the previous six days.

Regardless of our energy level, everyone made of flesh and blood requires rest, and God's Word addresses this.

God thought enough of relaxation to include it in the Ten Commandments, "Remember to observe the Sabbath day by keeping it holy. You have six days each week for your ordinary work, but the seventh day is a Sabbath day of rest dedicated to the LORD your God" (Exod. 20:8). Jesus, who was continually accused of doing good on the Sabbath, addressed it this way in Mark 2:27–28, "The Sabbath was made to meet the needs of the people, and not people to meet the requirements of the Sabbath. So the Son of Man is Lord, even over the Sabbath!"

The Sabbath was a time set aside to benefit people, to bring rest and wholeness to God's children. Obeying His commandment to rest is a form of worship, demonstrating to Him how much we honor His precepts; the inactivity of rest affords our bodies, minds, and spirits the opportunity to be renewed. We truly add the holy or sacred to Sabbath when we stop our normal activity and join with others to worship Him collectively as a congregation.

In addition, rest is not assigned to only one day each week. Solomon wrote, "It is useless for you to work so hard from early morning until late at night, anxiously working for food to eat; for God gives rest to his loved ones" (Ps. 127:2). For this reason, working 24/7 is not really a lifestyle to be admired.

Rest assured, great peace will come to our grassy hillside when we, His loved ones, nestle up to the Shepherd and rest.

Chapter 32

God Is in Control

Natural disasters befall rich and poor, young and old alike. These tragic events are a great common denominator that causes every victim to seek after the most basic needs—water, food, shelter, and clothing. Life is altered, and those who survive begin heading in a new direction, grateful to be alive.

A curious sheep followed the Shepherd on a scouting trip. The Shepherd was perusing a dry, rugged valley that would be tomorrow's journey. At first, the sheep did not mind the challenging surroundings because it was enthralled by the opportunity to venture off with the Shepherd. However, after a time, it began to focus on the difficulties of the journey, and bleated and grunted its complaints.

Suddenly the Shepherd put out His hand to silence the sheep and paused to listen to an approaching sound. In an instant, He gathered the sheep in His arms and climbed to a place of safety just as a heaving flashflood roared past them. As the unusual abundance of water settled into the valley, the Shepherd comforted His startled, shaking sheep and smiled to reassure it that all was well, He was in control.

The sheep witnessed an amazing act of God that day as the course of the flock was forever altered. This flooded valley was no longer a viable path for the flock, but tomorrow their Shepherd would provide a new direction for them—He is not threatened by catastrophe.

Before the flood, the sheep seemed to be complaining about everything. The road was rough and long, dry and barren. It did not appreciate the fact that the Shepherd was present, leading, and protecting. We tend to mimic the sheep's behavior when life gets a little rough, and often complain about all the little things that upset us. We seem to lack gratitude for all the good things we possess.

However, hurricanes and floods, fires and devastating storms become a reality check for us. It is amazing how precious a cool, clean cup of water becomes when we have nothing. How grateful we are for that water, so thankful to be alive! Our Shepherd is looking out for us!

Even though the flash flood altered its course, the sheep was spared from injury or death, safe in the arms of the Shepherd. Unfortunately, all are not spared from the storms that wreak havoc on the earth and some may perish. If they are followers of God, they still find themselves in His arms, at an eternal destination.

When we walk with God, we are certain to view His terrifying power displayed at times. Psalm 46 dramatically portrays how our awesome God controls this vast world:

> God is our refuge and strength, always ready to help in times of trouble. So we will not fear, when earthquakes come...mountains crumble...nations are in chaos...kingdoms crumble...God's voice thunders and the earth melts!...Be still, and know that I am God! The LORD of Heaven's Armies is here among us.

And tomorrow God will provide a new direction for us. He is not threatened by catastrophe; all is well. God is in control!

Chapter 33

TRULY FREE

SOCIETY HAS LED US TO BELIEVE THAT SOMETHING WILD and carefree is a good thing. Expressions such as wild party, wild flower, wild life, wild card, wild and woolly denote excitement without rules. We are told that a life without rules equals freedom—freedom to be me, freedom to choose what I will. This, however, is not consistent with the perception of freedom held by the Founding Fathers of the United States.

Although the very formation of our country was based on freedom, one of our first official documents, the U.S. Constitution, was a list of rules by which to govern it. And so we ask, what does it mean to be free?

One peaceful day, the Shepherd stretched out on a sandy hill along the seashore taking in the beauty of creation as the sheep grazed in the surrounding fields and cliffs. Suddenly an increasing vibration of the earth beneath Him broke the serenity, and He sat up. Looking toward the top of one of the hills, He saw His most trustworthy sheep nod, as if in affirmation of approaching danger.

The Shepherd quickly called His flock to join him, and they took shelter under a large overhang just as a herd of wild horses, loud and raucous, thundered over them and sent rocks flying. A few of the sheep trembled with fear, while other seasoned followers remained calm. However, some were mesmerized by the excitement of the wild horses and imagined what it would be like to enjoy the *freedom* they possessed.

When the dust settled, the wise Shepherd disarmed their thoughts and said, "The horses appear to be free, but in reality they are bound by the struggle to survive, running here and there in search of food, water, and shelter from the storms. They are never truly at rest. They were born, not to be wild and aimless, but rather to be loved and protected by those they serve. Once they are found and allowed to fulfill their destinies, then they will truly be free."

Untamed, uncultivated, unfarmed, unrefined, unsophisticated, uncultured, and undomesticated—these are terms linked to the definition of the word *wild*. They're not that appealing. We never hear bragging about attending an uncultured event or introduce a fun new unsophisticated friend. Yet, *wild* sounds so exciting.

In Luke 15:11–32, Jesus shared a story that teaches us about the true meaning of freedom. A young man, like some of the sheep, was mesmerized by the excitement of freedom. After acquiring his inheritance from his father, the son left home and lived a wild, fun-filled life without restrictions. Soon his fortune and friends were gone, and the Jewish young man found himself feeding pigs. Unsophisticated, uncultured, unrefined, unhappy, he was bound by the need to find water, food, and shelter—amenities his father had always provided. The dream of fulfilling his destiny in life was far from his thoughts.

Everyone has heard the "call of the wild" at one time or another and that is no disgrace. The Shepherd did not condemn the sheep, but instead, He encouraged them to continue following Him. Proverbs 29:18 teaches, "When people do not accept divine guidance, they run wild. But whoever obeys the law is joyful." Without the Shepherd's direction, we waste our lives pursuing all the unattractive "un's" of the wild; but with His loving and protecting guidance, we are free to happily fulfill His destiny for our lives. We are *free at last*!

Chapter 34
THE ANTIDOTE TO PANIC

THROAT CLOSES, PULSE ACCELERATES, STOMACH CHURNS, heart pounds, breathing quickens, head spins—these are well-known indicators of a panic attack. Whether it is produced by real or imagined events, high anxiety is as debilitating as it sounds and the physical ramifications are often long-term and more than just a nuisance. However, there is a way to avoid it.

A distant but thunderous noise caught the attention of the flock as they followed the Shepherd along the path. When they realized that He was leading them toward the sound, their pace automatically slackened—fear of the unknown is a powerful emotion. Soon, however, they stopped at the bank of a rough, raging river that was announcing its presence with a deafening roar. The Shepherd moved toward a bridge that appeared to be inadequate for passage over the rough waters. Yet He led them with great confidence, and many moved closer to Him so they could hear His words of comfort and instruction.

Meanwhile some of the sheep began to panic, and in their haste to cross over the threatening river, they pushed several others into the water. In spite of the resulting commotion, all but one of the waterlogged sheep was able to get safely to one shore or the other. As this one terrified sheep was swept down the raging river, struggling to stay afloat, it was too focused on its peril to notice the Shepherd running alongside it on the shore.

When the desperate sheep finally took its eyes off the river, it saw the crook of the Shepherd's staff extended over the water, ready to pull it to safety. However, it was still struggling and thrashing about, making it impossible for the Shepherd to get the hook around it; "Calm down," the Shepherd called out. "Don't panic. Let Me rescue you." As the sheep finally heeded this advice, the Shepherd was able to pull it safely onto the shore; great relief swept over the exhausted flock.

It appears that the Shepherd led His flock right into a crisis situation. Or did He? For some of the sheep, *anxiety*—worry about what may happen—had its beginning with the rumble in the distance. It grew to *panic*—a sudden unreasoning fear—at the sight of the raging river. And for one poor sheep, it became a full-blown panic attack with heart pounding and head swimming. From the very beginning, however, the Shepherd never stopped leading and guiding the flock on the path to their destination that day. He was neither anxious nor panicked about the river—it was not a crisis.

Many people feel that they live every moment of every day on the edge of a crisis, and this belief, whether real or imagined, affects how they respond to life's ordinary events. It is interesting to observe how a simple *bump* on a leg can actually begin to look more a *lump*, and in no time at all be imagined as a *stump*.[1] Perhaps we can overcome this tendency to panic and sudden, unreasoning fear by focusing on the behavior of our Shepherd. He is neither anxious nor panicked by our situation, and He will continue to lead and guide us to our destination.

Our Shepherd desires that we ignore the anxiety-producing sounds and sights and meditate instead on His written words of comfort. Rather than being known as people who always expect disaster, we can be known by the description of Psalm 112:6–7: "Those who are righteous will be long remembered. They do not fear bad news; they confidently trust the LORD to care for them."

The sheep that was being swept down the rapid river had reason for concern, but panic did not serve it well. David could certainly identify with the sheep's dilemma, and he was anxious, if not panicked, when he wrote in Psalm 69:1–2, "Save me, O God, for the floodwaters are up to my neck. Deeper and deeper I sink into the mire; I can't find a foothold. I am in deep water, and the floods overwhelm me." In the midst of his trouble, David called out to God to save him. "Rescue me, O God, by your saving power" (v. 29).

Sometimes God has to wait for us to get out of the way before He can save us. As this scenario shows, the Shepherd rescued the sheep when it stopped trying to save itself and turned to Him. Today, our Shepherd is calling to us, "Calm down, don't panic, and let Me rescue you."

Chapter 35

FATAL ATTRACTION

SOME PEOPLE POSSESS AN INNATE ABILITY TO CAPTIVATE others. We sometimes see a small baby who has had little opportunity to develop its personality, and remark, "Now, there's a real charmer!" When we shop by television, we meet magnetic personalities who are able to effortlessly influence us to buy their kitchen gadgets and health helps because we absolutely need them to make a better meal or be a better person.

We also meet them at the car lot, the insurance office—and yes, even in the church. On the latter occasion it will prove beneficial, before we blindly follow a deadly path, to remember the old adage, if it sounds too good to be true, it is.

One day, a *different* shepherd came amongst the flock. His appearance was somewhat rougher than that of the Shepherd; but his voice was unbelievably alluring. Before long, he had completely captivated a young sheep with his charisma, as he petted it and fawned over it.

Without warning, the Shepherd stepped into the scenario and pulled the lamb away from the charmer. The lamb immediately recognized the voice of His Shepherd as He spoke with authority, "The lamb is Mine!" As the naïve lamb rejoined the flock, it looked back with regret as the unknown shepherd reached out for it.

As soon as the lamb was out of sight, the intruder revealed his true intention. Throwing off his robe, he exposed himself as a thief searching for his dinner.

The smooth operator was a thief! Obviously, following the Good Shepherd does not eliminate the threat of a thief coming into our midst. A thief desires to take things that are not his and possess them. The craftiest of thieves is able to do this in full view of the victim, and not be perceived until it is too late. It was a close call for the lamb.

In a perfect world, an enemy who longs to devour our souls would not exist; however, our perfect world has not yet come.

Whether we are young or old, a new or seasoned follower, we have an enemy who desires to take things that are not his. He has been skillfully practicing his profession a long time, and the Apostle Peter warned the early church, both the elders and the young, "Be careful—watch out for attacks from Satan, your great enemy. He prowls around like a hungry roaring lion, looking for some victim to tear apart" (1 Pet. 5:8, TLB).

The little lamb was neither careful nor watchful for an attack from its enemy; in fact, an intruder that only resembled his Shepherd mesmerized it by simply making it feel good. Our enemy is adept in this same technique, and he desires much more from us than the purchase of a useless kitchen gadget. A different shepherd—a false shepherd—may come along with alluring words and snatch us away from the Lord before we realize it.

Paul spoke of this in 2 Timothy 4:3, "For a time is coming when people will no longer listen to sound and wholesome teaching. They will follow their own desires and will look for teachers who will tell them whatever their itching ears want to hear." The thief will speak a message that tickles our ears and promises a convenient relationship with God without restrictions or discipline, a way of life that always makes us feel good. In time, we become just like the shepherd we follow—devoured—because we failed to carefully watch out for the cunning attacks of our enemy.

But we do not have to succumb to this fatal attraction. Instead, we can enjoy the safety of close relationship with the Shepherd, as Psalm 68:19–20 describes it: "Praise the Lord; praise God our savior! For each day he carries us in his arms. Our God is a God who saves! The Sovereign LORD rescues us from death." Fortunately, the Shepherd does not easily let go of His sheep; when we, like the lamb, recognize Him as our Shepherd and respond to His conviction, He carries us away from our demise despite our temptation to stay.

Knowing us as He does, our Shepherd warns us in John 10:10, "The thief's purpose is to steal, kill and destroy. My purpose is to give life in all its fullness" (TLB). He understands what is necessary to achieve a full life because He created us. He knows what we want, but He also knows what we need—something that would not really concern a thief who desires to make us his lunch. When we find ourselves drawn to someone whose promises sound contrary to the clearly revealed truth of God's Word, we must break away from that fatal attraction and find safety in our Shepherd's arms.

Chapter 36

A Circle of Protection

IN THE EARLY HISTORY OF THE UNITED STATES, WAGON trains carried groups of settlers across the country to their new homes. Strong friendships were formed as together the pioneers faced many perils, including the opposition of hostile natives who were defending their homeland. When an attack was imminent, the wagon master would call the travelers to position their wagons in a circle in an attempt to save their lives. They placed everything that was dear to them inside the circle—a circle of protection.

Sensing an approaching storm, the Shepherd called the grazing flock to come to Him. In response, the sheep banded together in a tight circle around Him with their heads down, facing inward.

Within moments, a forceful windstorm with dirt and debris swirled past them and left a deposit of dirt, twigs, and leaves on the woolly sheep. However, none had been blinded or choked by the thick debris because they had banded together and brought protection to one another.

The countryside afforded neither barn nor shelter for the sheep to take refuge, yet when the windstorm passed their way, the unity of bringing their woolly bodies together in a circle around the Shepherd protected their heads, their most vulnerable part. Unity is a powerful thing.

Deliverance from the storm began when the flock obeyed the Shepherd's command. When life's storms threaten us, our deliverance will also begin with obedience to our Shepherd's command:

> When you obey me, you are living in my love, just as I obey my Father and live in his love.…I demand that you love each other as much as I love you. And here is how to measure it—the greatest love is shown when a person lays down his life for his friend.
>
> —John 15:10, 12–13, TLB

We may express many different kinds of love. For example, love between friends is conditioned on similar interests, love within a family thrives as long as a family unit exists, and sensual love is contingent on gratification. However, the laying-down-our-lives kind of agape love results from our obedience to God and is an eternal love for others. When we lack the latter kind of love for someone, we need to examine if we are also lacking in our obedience to God. Obedience and love, love and obedience—it is like a ring with no beginning and no end, a circle of protection.

The flock's deliverance was *secured* when the sheep banded *together* around the Shepherd and thus protected one another. In Matthew 18:19–20, Jesus explained to His disciples that power is unleashed when even two or three are in agreement, "I also tell you this: If two of you agree here on earth concerning anything you ask, my Father in heaven will do it for you. For where two or three gather together as my followers, I am there among them."

It is interesting to note that in the scriptures preceding this passage, Jesus gave the guidelines to resolve personal conflicts within the body of believers. It is also noteworthy that in the scriptures following it, Peter asked Jesus about forgiveness: "'Lord, how often should I forgive someone who sins against me? Seven times?' 'No, not seven times,' Jesus replied, 'but seventy times seven!'" (vv. 21–22). Jesus understood that conflict and unforgiveness threaten the power of agreement.

We are imperfect souls. When conflicts arise between us, it is helpful to remember that God loves each of us with an eternal love and has mapped out a path for each individual life. When we ask for mercy for our offenders, He gives mercy to us when we offend others. Because unresolved conflicts threaten our unity and make us vulnerable to life's storms, the Shepherd calls us to band together in love and forgiveness. He calls us to circle our wagons when the storms of life threaten us. In this circle of protection we are invincible.

Chapter 31

A Name That Will Deliver

I DO. I PROMISE TO LOVE, CHERISH, AND PROTECT IN sickness and health. With words such as these, rings are exchanged. So often, however, promises and hearts are broken. For many, *promise* has become a sloppy little word used as a bargaining chip in a verbal agreement or in a rousing campaign speech. Promises are easy to make, but difficult to deliver. In fact, some subscribe to the philosophy of the little

French general, Napoleon, "If you wish to be a success in the world, promise everything, deliver nothing."[1] In such a cynical world, is it possible to trust anyone's promises, even the promises of God?

With a slow, halting gait, the injured sheep walked close to the Shepherd. When a soft, grassy spot presented itself, the Shepherd called the flock to a halt, and the wounded sheep lay down with a painful wince. The Shepherd tore strips from His undergarment and securely wrapped them around the injured area as He spoke words of hope and promise. This provided under-girding strength and relief to the injured sheep as they proceeded together. Although the strips of fabric did not heal the sheep, they gave the promise of healing to come.

When the time was right, the Shepherd removed the strips, and the sheep darted about. It was healed and free to join the rest of the flock. However, it had grown accustomed to that secure place with Him, and it never strayed far.

It is important that we, like the injured sheep, trust in the Shepherd's promises. Although the Shepherd did not provide instantaneous healing for His injured sheep, He applied bandages that were promises of healing to come. The sheep carried these promises as it traveled on the road with the Shepherd. It never ran off in an attempt to heal itself or in protest about the time it spent waiting on the promise.

Abraham, the father of the nation of Israel, received a promise from God, "Then the LORD brought Abram outside beneath the night sky and told him, 'Look up into the heavens and count the stars if you can. Your descendants will be like that—too many to count!'" (Gen.15:5, TLB). While standing at the threshold of this promise, Abraham, at the bidding of his barren wife, attempted to fulfill it on his own by producing a son with a foreign substitute.

In spite of this, a merciful Lord spoke to the doubting couple in Genesis 18:14 and asked, "Is anything too hard for the Lord?" Within one year, Sarah gave birth to Isaac, the beginning of their starry sky. "The Lord... did for Sarah exactly what he had promised. She became pregnant, and she gave birth to a son for Abraham in his old age. This happened at just the time God had said it would" (Gen. 21:1–2, emphasis added).

However, their earlier act of impatience in failing to wait on God's promise brought about a nation that has been in conflict with Israel every since. Perhaps God included this account of Abraham's failure in the Bible not only for its historical value, but also as a lesson on the virtue of waiting for God to fulfill His promises.

God has given us over 1,200 written promises in the Bible, not to mention those He whispers to our hearts. One of them is Isaiah 40:31:

> Those who trust in the LORD will find new strength. They will soar high on wings like eagles. They will run and not grow weary. They will walk and not faint.

As the above scenario shows, the sheep not only found healing in due time, but it also enjoyed the undergirding strength from the Shepherd's promises as it waited.

When we grow impatient waiting for the fruition of God's

promise and are tempted to cut and run, we must consider the One who made the promise to us. David expressed this confidence in Psalm 138:2, when he wrote: "I praise your name for your unfailing love and faithfulness, for your *promises* are backed by all the honor of your name" (emphasis added). The name of God is a name that will deliver.

Chapter 38

Victory Over Terror

My heart pounds in my chest. The terror of death assaults me. Fear and trembling overwhelm me, and I can't stop shaking.

—Psalm 55:4–5, emphasis added

THIS CRY OF DAVID IS AN APT DESCRIPTION OF OUR feelings on September 11, 2001, as we were awakened to the knowledge that our country would never be the same.

We had been violated, body, soul, and spirit, and our innocence has been lost. David's words, which he uttered centuries before as he faced death at the hand of his enemy, illustrate the fact that terror is ancient.

The sunny blue sky brought beauty and warmth to the day as the Shepherd led the flock up a gentle incline. At the top of the rise, He came to an abrupt halt to view an expansive pasture filled with bushes and shrubs and a tall, distinctive tree. It was not so unusual for Him to stop throughout the journey each day to pause for the stragglers to catch up, but this time He did not look back at the flock. Even when the sheep came from behind nudging and bumping Him, the Shepherd kept His eyes fixed on the sky before Him.

Suddenly, in a split second, the sun-drenched spectators were stunned as a thunderous black cloud rolled up in front of them. They watched in amazement as the storm released a lightning bolt that struck the tall tree and immediately filled the air with black smoke and flying debris.

After a time, the Shepherd led the shaken flock down the gradual slope to the smoky pasture ahead. As they passed by the tree, the sheep watched in horror as it crumbled to a heap of ashes right before their eyes. They had never witnessed an act with such destructive force, and it terrified them. The acrid odor from the terrifying fire lingered in their nostrils for many days. They became more watchful, more dependent on the guidance of their Shepherd should another storm lie ahead.

The flock was not unfamiliar with tragedy. It had seen the devastation left in the aftermath of storms on many occasions, but it had never encountered one quite like this. It was sudden, precise, destructive, and close. No doubt, many from the flock wondered why their Shepherd would allow them to witness such a horrific display.

After September 11, speculation over the cause of the terrifying attack ran rampant. Why would a loving God allow it? Did He cause it as punishment for our nation's sins? Where was He, and what was He thinking? Fortunately, God is neither threatened nor offended by our questions, but we may delay our own understanding of events when we attempt to answer these questions *for* Him. In Romans 11:34 Paul wrote, "For who can know the LORD's thoughts? Who knows enough to give him advice?" In light of this, the more important question to ask is now that God has our attention, what might He be saying to us?

Just as the Shepherd led the flock closely past the crumbling tree, our televisions brought the collapsing Trade Center right into our living rooms. As we sat and watched the unfolding news coverage, the parameters of that square box disappeared, and we felt as if we were choking on the ash and debris right alongside the victims. In some small measure, we felt their pain. In this empathy, perhaps God is saying that we should look around us. Each day we rub shoulders with at least one hurting soul who is experiencing a personal 911—a broken heart, a broken home, a broken body. A friendly smile, a kind word, or a heartfelt prayer could make all the difference in the life of one who is facing tragedy.

At the September 11 memorial service, President George

Bush spoke the comforting words, "Grief and tragedy and hatred are only for a time. Goodness, remembrance and love have no end, and the Lord of life holds all who die and all who mourn."[1] We, a more *watchful* nation, have left the smoldering pasture and hopefully we are more alert to our neighbor's sorrow and always ready to comfort the brokenhearted.

Since September 11, every individual faces the challenge of living a more cautious life without succumbing to fear. While the horrific events of that day were evil, even more malevolent was the intent of the attackers to change a peaceful, secure nation into one overcome with fear, horror, dread, shock, fright, panic, and alarm. Although the passage of time has lessened the impact of these characteristics of terror, it revisits us through anthrax, explosive shoes, and verbal threats by our enemies. Everyday events that at one time caused only a small measure of distress, may now produce exaggerated reactions because of the subliminal fear lurking within us. When we live in fear, *terror wins*.

When Jesus, the Good Shepherd, returned to heaven 2,000 years ago, He sent His Spirit to shepherd us on life's path. Already aware of September 11 and all the terrors to come, He comforted His followers shortly before He departed, "I am leaving you with a gift—peace of mind and heart. And the peace I give is a gift the world cannot give. So don't be troubled or afraid" (John 14:27).

Jesus is offering the same gift of *peace*—the absence of fear, horror, dread, shock, fright, panic, and alarm—to His followers today. Take this gift and don't be afraid, He says. It is not given to those who follow the peace conveyed through the words of the media, the politicians, and the bloggers.

Rather, it is a peace given to all those who follow Him and are comforted by *His* Word, regardless of threatening storms ahead. When we live in His peace, *terror loses.*

Chapter 39

INSIGNIFICANT DIFFERENCES

PREJUDICE—INTOLERANCE AND HATRED BASED ON SKIN color, affluence, political affiliation, and many other things—lurks within every people group on every continent. Through the centuries, war and bloodshed have not solved the swelling tide of prejudice around the world. It causes one to question in exasperation, "Can't we all just get along?"

The Shepherd's flock was comprised of many different breeds of sheep, and most of them traveled together along the journey. However, some that were similar in appearance and mannerisms tended to travel in individual groups. It was difficult to distinguish if they had alienated themselves from the others or if the others had alienated them.

One day a group that was dark faced and somewhat large surrounded the Shepherd as He walked, and many of the other sheep kept their distance. In His arms, the Shepherd carried a white wooly lamb that was fidgeting and looked increasingly *uncomfortable* as they traveled. It was unusual for a lamb to do this when it was in the Shepherd's arms, but perhaps it needed its mother or desired to travel in its own group. As the Shepherd put the fidgeting lamb down, the earth began to shake. For a few seconds, the flock fell and rolled around on the quaking earth.

The earthquake made very little alteration to the physical scenery, but the landscape of the flock changed dramatically. The groups had disappeared. Dark-faced and white-faced sheep, short hair and long hair, small and large breeds were mixed together, nudging each other and bleating their concerns over what had just occurred. Their differences were insignificant in light of what they had just experienced together.

Genesis 1:27 declares, "So God created human beings in his own image. In the image of God he created them; male and female he created them." God created *people,* with the exclusion of no one, in the image of Himself—He was the prototype, with a body (His Son), a soul (His character), and a spirit (His Spirit).

Just as a newly designed car has a prototype with many colors and variations to follow, we are the many colors and variations that follow our Prototype. As it is with an automobile, neither the color nor the style makes us run, but what is under the hood—the spirit *inside* of us. How unfortunate that we so often stop at the color, the clothing, the politics of others and never look at the one thing that is identical in all of us—a spirit striving to connect with our Creator and His creation.

As it was with the flock, sometimes God allows *quakes* to shake us up. Catastrophic storms, floods, terrorism, and death cause us to realize, if only for a brief moment, that we are all in this together, nudging each other along in comfort. Do we need to have a tragedy or *crash* in our lives for us to follow God's *one simple rule* for our interactions with one another? Our Shepherd taught, "Do to others what you would have them to do to you, for this sums up the Law and the Prophets" (Matt. 7:12, NIV). It is noteworthy that the Shepherd did not tell us to follow this rule exclusive to our own race, socio-economic group, and political affiliation.

In the final hours of Jesus' life on earth, He prayed earnestly for His followers and said, "I pray that they will all be one, just as you and I are one—as you are in me, Father, and I am in you. And may they be in us so that world will believe you sent me" (John 17:21). The One who created all of us in His own likeness believes that we equally merit one another's kindness; and He desires that we live as *one* with each other and with Him. It seems then, that we will all get along just fine if we live as one colorful, spirit-centered creation and treat everyone else the way we desire to be treated.

Chapter 40

LESSONS FROM SUFFERING

WHEN WE ARE WRAPPED UP IN OUR OWN LITTLE worlds and fail to see the pain and suffering of others, it is like wearing a Kick Me sign on our backs. God sees it, and sometimes, because He loves us and desires to see us grow, He feels compelled to oblige.

Following the Shepherd does not mean that every day is filled with the bliss one would expect; in fact some days are actually quite painful. One such day, a limping sheep made its way to the Shepherd and began tugging on His garment to attract His attention. The Shepherd did not respond to the sheep, but continued to walk. Deeply disturbed by this, the sheep became desperate and its tugging changed to yanking and bleating. It did not realize that the Shepherd was looking for the best place to stop and minister to its needs.

Finally, the Shepherd halted the flock and sat on a nearby rock. The sheep, which by this time had latched onto His garments, lay at His feet. As the Shepherd mended its leg, He shared two valuable lessons with the ailing sheep. First, He explained that suffering produces compassion. They looked together at the vast flock, and, for the first time, the sheep observed many others with bandaged limbs and salve-covered wounds. Second, as He responded to the sheep's unwavering determination to receive healing, the Shepherd affirmed that persistence produces results. When the pair rejoined the flock that day, a wiser, more compassionate sheep followed the Shepherd.

Each day we rub shoulders with people who are suffering, those who have caused their suffering by their own hands and others who suffer through no fault of their own. Often we are just too busy to notice. If we do notice, we might make the serious mistake of wondering why they don't just snap out of it and move on. Just as a diseased heart requires medical attention, a calloused heart requires spiritual attention, and our Shepherd knows just the procedure to use.

Our hearts are softened when we endure suffering. Yes, the Shepherd could keep us from pain and stop our prolonged suffering. However, He often waits so He can be more gracious to us, giving us compassion for others. Sometimes the only opportunity we have to reach those who do not follow the Lord is through the compassion we show them when they suffer, compassion that developed in us through our own pain. The apostle Paul explained, "He comforts us in all our troubles so that we can comfort others. When others are troubled, we will be able to give them the same comfort God has given us" (2 Cor. 1:4).

The determined sheep learned through its suffering that persistence pays off. At the exact moment the Shepherd was ready to bring comfort, the sheep was at His feet, boldly latched on to His garment and ready for a miracle. The writer of Hebrews encourages us to do the same, "So let us come boldly to the throne of our gracious God. There we will receive his mercy, and we will find grace to help us when we need it most" (4:16).

Not all suffering is an object lesson for compassion and persistence. However, when we suffer, we would do well to examine the tenderness of our hearts toward others and also to measure our determination to reach God's throne for deliverance. When our suffering has ended, we will rejoin the flock a little wiser and a little more compassionate as we follow Him.

Chapter 41

Purely Motivated

Everyone enjoys attention. Some enjoy it more than others, even to the point that they live as actors who view the entire world as their stage. They are always seeking to be noticed by others, and this is exhausting—for the one who is seeking attention and for those whose attention is being sought.

As He led the flock on a journey through a somewhat mountainous area, the Shepherd stopped at the edge of a cliff. He placed His foot on one of the large rocks, rested His elbow on His knee, and with His chin on His hand, surveyed the area. The approaching flock saw the cliff and instinctively backed away—all except a lamb that moved right up to the cliff's edge. No doubt it viewed this as an opportunity to enjoy the full attention of the Shepherd and the rest of the flock.

Suddenly, the earth beneath the lamb began to give way. The other sheep halted all other movement and looked to the Shepherd to save the lamb from falling. However, He did not. When the lamb had dropped out of sight, He moved to the edge of the cliff and looked down to where it now lay motionless. Calling the other sheep to follow Him, He led them on a winding path down the mountain to the lamb. As the flock gathered around Him, the saddened Shepherd began to stroke the lamb. Soon its eyes began to flutter open, and the Shepherd tended to its injuries and scooped it up.

The Shepherd carried the lamb close to His heart for many days while its injuries healed. During this time, the little lamb began to understand the heart of the Shepherd as it listened, up close and personal, to His words of wisdom. After a while, the lamb was well enough to walk on its own, and no longer sought the attention of others. It pursued the Shepherd out of a profound love for Him, knowing that His attention was but a heartbeat away.

Like the lamb, young people are notorious for seeking attention. Our children are the most mischievous when our attention is diverted elsewhere, and this cry for attention often leads to poor behavior. For some teenagers, body piercing, tattoos, and black leather are a passing fad; but for all too many, this behavior is a cry for attention. They may not receive the kind of attention they truly seek, but at least they will be noticed.

Unfortunately, this need for attention is not limited to adolescence. It often motivates our actions as adults too, and it may be why we do the things we do. Loud, raucous behavior and seductive clothing are obvious attention-getters, but good deeds and gift-giving are too. Why do we help the poor, give great gifts, and prepare wonderful meals? Is our behavior driven by a desire to bless others or is it driven by the need to receive the kudos and attention it affords? It's a question of motives—why we do the things we do.

When Paul wrote to the church in Corinth, he used the example of a builder's workmanship to caution the believers about faulty motives:

> But there is going to come a time of testing at Christ's Judgment Day to see what kind of material each builder has used. Everyone's work will be put through the fire so that all can see whether or not it keeps its value and what was really accomplished. Then every workman...whose work still stands, will get his pay. But if the house he has built burns up, he will have great loss. He himself will be saved, but like a man escaping through a wall of flames.
>
> —1 Corinthians 3:13–15, TLB

In light of this, we, like David, should daily cry out, "Put me on trial, LORD, and cross-examine me. Test my motives and my heart" (Ps. 26:2). Then, when our actions are eternally judged, we will not suffer loss.

The motivation of the needy lamb changed when it began a close relationship with the Shepherd and learned why He does the things He does. The lamb no longer acted out of a need for attention from others because it had all it needed from the Shepherd and pursued Him, purely motivated by love. In a similar way, our motives will be transformed by a close relationship with our Shepherd. We will no longer act out of a need for attention but will perform acts of goodness, purely motivated by His love.

James 3:17–18 teaches:

> But the wisdom from above is first of all pure. It is also peace loving, gentle at all times, and willing to yield to others. It *is full of mercy and good deeds*. It shows no favoritism and is *always sincere*. And those who are peacemakers will plant seeds of peace and reap a harvest of righteousness.

As we pursue the Lord and His wisdom rather than momentary attention, we will find the motive for all this goodness is but His heartbeat away.

Chapter 42

FOLLOW THE LEADER

IN OUR "MOVERS AND SHAKERS" WORLD OF TODAY, HUGE groups of people pay large sums of money to hear one individual share the keys to great leadership. In their quest for knowledge, it is very important that these potential leaders discover this one simple statement, "Whoever wants to be a leader among you must be your servant" (Matt. 20:26).

As the large flock followed the Shepherd, it was obvious that some of the sheep were influential leaders and that the other sheep looked to them for direction. On this particularly difficult travel day, uncertainty among the leading sheep was causing delay and confusion for some of the flock.

Many of the leaders were focusing on the challenges of the present situation—the difficult terrain, the threats from howling wolves and the increasing winds. They were not serving the flock well, and their leadership slowed down the progress of the flock by causing fear and hesitancy. However, the flock also included leaders that watched the Shepherd's every move, unaffected by the circumstances. These wise leaders brought confidence, peace, and sure steps for the sheep that looked to them for direction. Ever mindful of those they led, they nudged and encouraged the followers along, just like the Shepherd had often demonstrated.

The Shepherd called the flock to a halt and began to walk among the sheep, calling forward the trustworthy leaders, indicating to the rest of the flock the leadership that would best *serve* them.

The Old Testament gives generous coverage to the lives of King Saul and King David. These two influential Jewish leaders took contrasting approaches to leadership, and thereby illustrated a significant lesson about it—when our leadership focus is determined by anything other than the direction of the Lord, we fail to serve the best interests of those whom we lead.

King Saul was "the most handsome man in Israel—head and shoulders taller than anyone else in the land" (1 Sam. 9:2). Unfortunately, good looks do not make a leader. Throughout his reign, Saul's leadership was a continual reaction to his circumstances rather than an obedient response to the directives of Samuel, the man of God. The Book of 1 Samuel records Saul's reaction to the difficulty and threats of battle that led him to offer an illegal sacrifice; to disobey God's direction by sparing the lives of his enemies; and to withhold food from his troops, causing them to sin by eating impure meat. (See 1 Samuel 13:9–4; 15:1–23; 14:24–32.)

Saul lost his kingdom because of his many offenses, even offering an excuse for each of them. In his parting words to Samuel, ever mindful of the increasing winds against him, Saul pleaded, "Please, at least honor me before the elders of my people and before Israel by coming back with me so that I may worship the LORD your God" (1 Sam. 15:30). Somewhere along the line, Saul's leadership became all about him and his circumstances when it should have been about God and serving His people.

Although King David was far from perfect, he was, as God described him, "a man after my own heart" (Acts 13:22). David was endeared to God because he was totally dependent on Him. When the difficulty of the battle closed in around him and the circumstances of life threatened, David's responses emanated from this sole belief, "The LORD is my shepherd; I have all that I need" (Ps. 23:1).

David made mistakes during this reign, serious mistakes, but instead of making excuses for them, the paradigm he gave his followers was that of repentance. A high point of his exemplary life was the time he danced in worship before the Lord and before all God's people when the Ark of the Covenant was returned to Jerusalem. (See 2 Samuel 6:14–15.) He was not worried about image, as Saul had been. He was not concerned about where he stood in the polls but gave himself in joyful abandonment to God, his Shepherd. David served God's people well.

Our leader, the Shepherd, set the example for leaders while He was here on this earth. As a leader, Jesus clearly illustrated where His focus was. In John 5:19, He said, "I tell you the truth, the Son can do nothing by himself. He does only what he sees the Father doing. Whatever the Father does, the Son also does." He did not react to polls or focus groups, but simply followed His Father.

Born in a stable with no home to call His own, yet the very Son of God, Jesus declared:

> Whoever wants to be a leader among you must be your servant, and whoever wants to be first among you must become your slave. For even the Son of Man came not to be served but to serve others and to give his life as a ransom for many.
>
> —Matthew 20:26–28

Jesus sacrificially demonstrated this simple statement that a leader is a servant to all.

The Shepherd's trustworthy leaders remained unhampered because they kept their focus on the Shepherd while they navigated the difficult terrain and endured the increasing winds. They led by following His example. This is the core principle of "Leadership Training 101": Follow the Leader and serve those you lead.

Chapter 43

AN UNSAFE VENTURE

CURIOSITY IS NOT NECESSARILY BAD. IN ALL PROBability, it is the trigger that leads to most great discoveries and inventions. However, no matter how noble it may be, curiosity has the potential of leading us down a path to discoveries that are not so great.

It was late in the day when a curious ram wandered away from the flock to see what was on top of a distant hill. When he arrived, he discovered that the top was simply a pile of jagged rocks and shrubs, hardly worth the climb. In his attempt to return to the safety of the flock, his leg became wedged between two sharp rocks. The jagged rocks cut him as he struggled and twisted in vain to release the leg. He began to shake with fear—he was stuck, bleeding, with night approaching and the wind mounting. He bleated loudly for help until he was hoarse and could no longer call out.

All of a sudden he saw the Shepherd come over the hill, silhouetted by the setting sun, His garments flying in the wind. When all hope was gone, the Shepherd had found him. The Shepherd gently eased his leg from the rocks, and spoke words of comfort as He mended the cuts. Then He sat and cradled him in His arms until he stopped shaking. He comforted the ram, "Surely by now you know that I would never abandon you."

When they returned to the flock, the ram rejoined the flock. The sheep were relieved, for the lost had been found. He was safely back to the fold, curious no longer.

It was not wise for the ram to venture away from the Shepherd to climb up a mountain just to see what was there. Such unhealthy curiosity may take us on a journey to a dangerous destination before we consider the consequences. Wisdom would have counseled the sheep to stay home. It was late in the day, and it was foolish to go off alone on an unknown path. If the Shepherd considered the mountain a worthy place to go, He would lead the flock there.

Curiosity may cause us to venture into unsafe territory. Just how fast can this car go? What exactly is on that Web site? Would two pills be better than one? How does it feel to . . . ? Dozens of questioning thoughts cross our minds each day, and most of them do not involve the discovery of a new wonder drug. We need wisdom to sort out those thoughts that could lead to a painful outcome. In Proverbs, Solomon gave his son an excellent explanation on how to receive this wisdom:

> Tune your ears to wisdom, and concentrate on understanding. Cry out for insight, and ask for understanding. Search for them as you would for silver; seek them like hidden treasures. Then you will understand what it means to fear the LORD, and you will gain knowledge of God. For the LORD grants wisdom! From his mouth come knowledge and understanding. He grants a *treasure of common sense* to the honest. He is a shield to those who walk with integrity. He guards the paths of the just and protects those who are faithful to him. Then you will understand what is right, just, and fair, and you will find the right way to go. For wisdom will enter your heart, and knowledge will fill you with joy. Wise choices will watch over you. Understanding will keep you safe.
>
> —Proverbs 2:2–11, emphasis added

As followers of the Shepherd, we know that even in our *lack* of wisdom, we will, just like the ram, find Him coming over *our* hill, His garments flying, responding to our call for help. Sometimes the measure of pain is great, but He comforts us in His arms, mends our wounds, and returns us to safety, a little wiser and *curious no longer.*

Chapter 44

LEFT OUT IN THE COLD

Photo credit: Barbara Cassell

NIGHT NEVER REALLY COMES AS A SURPRISE. THE lowering sun on the horizon brings darkness, atmospheric changes produce a chill in the air, and the Shepherd's voice calls the sheep to the fold. Throughout the countryside, however, so many are left out in the cold. Why don't they follow the Shepherd? Why don't they come to the fold?

The sheep were scattered over many hills as a beautiful sun set in the western sky. Many sheep looked up at the colorful sunset and saw the Shepherd's silhouette beckoning them to come home to the fold. Those who first saw Him started toward the gate, nudging others to follow under the darkening sky. However, as they looked back it was apparent that many were not coming. The hill to the Shepherd was steep in places and perhaps they felt it was too difficult to climb. They just stopped.

As the sky turned black, those who had reached the Shepherd realized that the other sheep could no longer see Him. Now it was too late to come. Why hadn't they followed?

Empty pews once filled with smiling faces often cause us to wonder what has happened. A little family once sat in that pew Sunday after Sunday, and now it is empty. The single woman who cried a lot during each service is gone, and the quiet couple that sat on the next to the last row has missed two, maybe three months. Why have they stopped coming?

Many people start out on the path to God, but because of discouragement or difficulties, they just stop. They hardly know Him, and no one seems to be concerned about them—until they're gone. The shepherd of our church flock does his best to contact them and encourage them to come, but we who rub shoulders with them at church, in the neighborhood, or on the job have the greatest impact. We should be ever mindful that it is nearly impossible to encourage those who are going through a rough time if we are too busy judging them for not being at church, or if we are so intently engaged in our own world that we fail to see their struggle.

When the writer of Psalm 43 was going through a time of deep discouragement, he prayed in verse 3, "Send out your light and your truth; let them guide me. Let them lead me to your holy mountain, to the place where you live." Jesus taught His followers in Matthew 5:14, "You are the *light* of the world" (emphasis added). Light catches the attention of people, and we must therefore charge up our lights and carry His truth, seeking out those who need encouragement to follow the Shepherd. We just may be the answer to someone's prayer for help. As we are reminded by the wisest man who ever lived, *"He who wins souls is wise"* (Prov. 11:30, NIV, emphasis added).

At times, we, too, may find ourselves in a position of discouragement. We may feel left out in the cold and may cry, "Nobody cares. Nobody likes me." It is risky to allow our destiny to be determined by someone else's failure to care. It is so much better to run, not walk, to the Shepherd who will save our lives. This, too, is wise.

Chapter 45

THE GATEKEEPER

PUSHING, SHOVING, FALLING DOWN—ONE MIGHT EXPECT these terms to illustrate a football game in progress, but they often explain the behavior of the football fans who are endeavoring to get into the stadium. Once the gates open, everyone tries to enter at the same time and find a place in the bleachers. It seems that they're almost like sheep. A better-organized, more orderly plan is to queue the attendees and place a gatekeeper in the middle of the gate to take tickets from both sides.

Night was advancing across the countryside, and the sheep, tired and ready for rest, rushed past the Shepherd to the fold. As the Shepherd approached the fold, He found a bottleneck at the somewhat narrow gate as the sheep pushed and jostled to move through it. The Shepherd moved to the middle of the gateway and stood there, allowing the sheep to pass one by one on either side of Him safely into the fold.

Although it would seem that His position at the gate would narrow the passageway further, it actually brought order and safety to the flock. As the sheep passed by Him one by one, the Shepherd, who knew each one by name, was able to see who was there and who was not.

We might wonder if having many gates would allow more sheep to enter the fold more quickly and find rest sooner. Jesus answered our questions about this. In John 10:7, 9, He declared, "I tell you the truth, I am the gate for the sheep... Yes I am the gate. Those who come in through me will be saved." In Matthew 7:13, He said, "Enter through the narrow gate. For wide is the gate and broad is the road that leads to destruction, and many enter through it" (NIV). He is the only way to heaven and clearly proclaimed, "I am the way, the truth and the life. No one can come to the Father except through me" (John 14:6).

None of our questions will change the facts. The Lord our

Shepherd was chosen by God to be the only gateway to eternity with Him. God, our creator, overflowing with great love for His lost creation, sent His Son to be our gateway to Him. All that He requires is that we accept this Savior and follow Him to His Father. Any other gate would be an insult and a mockery of God's sacrificial gift to us.

Order was not the only benefit the Shepherd gave the flock by positioning Himself in the gateway. He was a very *personal* shepherd, and He knew each one by name. Because of His familiarity with each sheep, the Shepherd knew immediately if one failed to pass by Him, and He would then search for the missing sheep.

Our God knows us by name too. In fact, He knows us so personally that He has actually numbered the hairs on our head. (See Matthew 10:30.) For those who are hair challenged, this may not be such a big deal, but for most of us, it screams intimacy—intimacy with our Creator. Although He will not force our devotion, He will pursue us and abundantly fill us with His love.

Bless the Gatekeeper!

Chapter 46

UNINVITED GUESTS

AFTER A LONG TRIP OR AN ENDLESS DAY AT WORK, THERE really is nothing like home sweet home. Because our homes are very important to our well-being, we go to great lengths to make them safe. We remove unwanted critters, insects, radon, lead, and asbestos; and we employ locks and bolts to protect us from uninvited guests who would choose to do us harm. However, these efforts are inadequate against even more menacing sources of danger that may be present in our four walls. For protection against the threat of such evil, we just may need to call the *Exterminator*.

As dusk approached, the Shepherd led the flock to the fold and stopped just outside the gate. He entered the fold alone and walked from corner to corner, searching for any harmful thing that may have entered while they were gone.

In the far corner the Shepherd found a large coiled snake hidden in the darkness. He lightly jabbed at the snake with His staff and then stepped back to observe. The snake, feeling the threat of exposure or harm, slithered out of the fold through the hole it had entered, and the wise Shepherd repaired the hole to prevent future visits from the adversary.

When the sheep entered the fold, the scent of the snake still lingered in the corner where it had been. At first they were reluctant to move into that corner, but eventually the sheep settled themselves throughout the fold, ever grateful for a Shepherd who went before them to remove danger from their home.

The promises in the first fourteen verses of Psalm 91 are some of the most comforting passages in the Bible:

> Those who *live* in the shelter of the Most High will find rest in the shadow of the Almighty....He will rescue you from every trap and protect you from deadly disease....He will shelter you with His wings....Do

> not be afraid of the terrors of the night.... I will protect those who trust in my name.
>
> —Psalm 91:1, 3–5, 14

This place of shelter is where we desire to live, safe, protected, and free from fear and anxiety.

Unfortunately, our homes are not always worry-free places of refuge. All too often we are plagued with stomach-churning anxiety or have children who are tormented by fearful dreams. A sense of dissatisfaction may invade our minds and our closest relationships. What has happened to home sweet home? Perhaps we need to ask the Shepherd to walk through our homes and search for any harmful things that may have come in without our knowledge. When He finds something that is harmful, we must allow Him to expose where it entered our dwelling.

Advanced technology has given us incredible devices to help us manage our homes, but it has also delivered dangerous sights and sounds into our living rooms through a neat little television or computer screen. We may not realize that uninvited guests, the philosophy and deeds of godless entertainment, are invading the corners of our hearts and minds, filling them with values contrary to the heart of the Shepherd. However, the repetitious digesting of horror, violence, and sexual promiscuity, no matter how neatly packaged, will eventually revisit us with fear, anxiety, and discontentment. Just as threatening are the myriad of television talk shows that encourage an empty all-about-me lifestyle and a music industry that fosters hopelessness and anger in our teens.

If we suspect that uninvited guests may be lurking within

our four walls, it is time to invite the Shepherd to go before us into our dwelling to find the harmful things and to expose their place of entry. Then, let us proclaim with David, "I will lead a life of integrity *in my own home*. I will refuse to look at anything vile and vulgar" (Ps. 101:2–3, emphasis added).

Under the Shepherd's protective guidance, we can have a safe home sweet home!

Chapter 41

HE'S GOT OUR BACK

WHEN WE CLOSE THE DOOR AT HOME EACH EVENING, WE have no idea what scenarios may unfold in the outside world. Each day, our television news is filled with violent acts and terrorism at home and around the world, and we do not know what tomorrow may bring. However, we do know that we follow a Shepherd who watches over us and guards what we cannot see—He's got our back.

Night was closing in, and the Shepherd led the sheep to the fold. As He opened the gate, they rushed past Him, anxious to get to safety. However, He did not follow them inside to rest. Instead, He secured the gate and began a slow walk around the fold. At the back of the fold, He discovered a hole in the wall—the enemy had been there while they were gone!

Without a second thought, the Shepherd reclined in front of the hole and remained there all night. When the wolves returned to harm the sheep, the *presence* of the Shepherd caused them to fade into the night, unsuccessful in their venture. What a wise Shepherd He is!

We, like the psalmist David, can say, "In *peace* I will lie down and sleep, for you alone, O LORD, will keep me safe" (Ps. 4:8, emphasis added). This was quite a statement for David to make considering the fact that he spent much of his life hunted by King Saul, his son Absalom, and many foreign enemies. Such confidence comes from faithfully following the Shepherd and from knowing His character. The alternative remedies of consuming pills and alcohol to buffer the uncertainty of our frightful days cannot mimic *peaceful* sleep, and they only provide an unsatisfying addicting remedy. Perhaps we should consider the old adage which tells us that God is going to be up all night anyway, so we might as well go to sleep and let Him do the worrying—and the protecting.[1]

Even in the daylight hours when we cannot see what is behind us, we can walk forward in confidence. Isaiah 58:8

promises, "Your godliness will lead you forward, and the glory of the Lord will protect you *from behind*" (emphasis added). In other words, the glory of the Lord, the *presence* or essence of God, will protect us from attacks that we cannot see as our godliness, or right living, leads us forward. It is difficult to understand how the children of Israel could trade this wonderful security of God's glory for a statue of a grass-eating ox. (See Psalm 106:20.) Hopefully, we will not trade His glory for anything.

In spite of the today's news reports and the constant threat of danger, we can find our security in God. We can go forward throughout the day and rest peacefully each night with this wonderful assurance—He's got our back!

Chapter 48

SHEAR HUMILIATION

MANY TIMES SUFFERING AND LOSS LEAVE US FEELING humiliated. We feel like Job who, when he was tested, said, "My days are over. My hopes have disappeared. My heart's desires are broken" (Job 17:11). However, God loves to bring good out of chaos—that is how He created the universe. This is aptly illustrated in the story of a small, ugly horse named Seabiscuit. Abuse and neglect seemed to disqualify him from ever accomplishing anything of value, yet today his name sits among princes in the Winners' Circle.[1] Yes, lives that have suffered pain and loss can still obtain greatness!

A lonely ewe rested on a little mound of grass far from the flock, cuddling in the long blades in an attempt to keep warm. She had been *sheared,* and in addition to feeling cold, she was embarrassed and humiliated. How could the Shepherd have allowed this! Alone and naked, the ewe was full of self-pity as she shivered in the cold night air.

The Shepherd appeared out of nowhere and beckoned her to come. Surely, she thought, He will embrace me and carry me home. However, He did not. Instead, He placed His hand on her head and guided her home to the fold.

When they reached the fold, the ewe stared in amazement at the spectacle before her. All the sheep had been sheared! After her hasty departure from being sheared, all the other sheep had experienced equal humiliation. Her desire to be carried home like a weak, pathetic sheep was selfish and wrong. No wonder the Shepherd insisted that she walk to the fold. He always had her best interests at heart.

Inside the fold, the ewe no longer felt the chill of the cold night air, but the warmth of the other sheep. She no longer felt naked and embarrassed; in fact, she felt right a home with the rest of the flock. She was not alone.

When the ewe was sheared, she never really understood what happened to her nor why because, in her humiliation, she left the Shepherd. As the saying goes, misery loves company, and the ewe would have found plenty of it that day if she had stuck around. Shearing, or fleecing, is a rough procedure that most sheep only endure because they are bound or held during the process. This is why the human connotation of being sheared or fleeced is so negative. To be sheared means being deprived of power, rank, or rights; and to be fleeced or swindled is equally damaging.

We, like the ewe, are tempted to run to a solitary place to lick our wounds after we are sheared. We are embarrassed and want to escape humiliation at the questioning looks of others who may wonder what happened and why. Everyone has been fleeced or sheared at one time or another, and usually more than once. Bad things happen to everyone—to the righteous and the wicked, to the influential and the humble. Some suffering occurs by our own hand, some at the hands of others, and some by the testing of the Lord; but regardless of how it comes, the heart of the issue is how we respond to them.

The Bible records that God considered Job to be the "finest man in all the earth" (Job 1:8), yet through testing, he was *sheared* of everything of value to him. His response to this loss seemed to run the gamut, but he never left the care of the Shepherd, even when his wife encouraged him to curse God and die. He endured endless criticism from friends, who, to be sure, were later humiliated when God rebuked them for their prideful counsel to Job. During the darkest days of his trial, Job confidently proclaimed, "I know that my Redeemer lives" (Job 19:25). In the end, God lifted Job out of all of the rubble and restored everything he had lost, and then some, after he prayed for his so-called friends.

One of our greatest enemies is the sense that we are not good enough to follow God because of the shame and humiliation we feel from past wrongs done *by* us or *to* us. We leave the fold to find a place of comfort, but we never really find it and never fulfill God's destiny for us this way. However, just as in the case of the sheared ewe, the Shepherd comes looking for us. Psalm 113:6–8 says, "He stoops to look.... He lifts the poor from the dust and the needy from the garbage dump. He set them among princes, even the princes of His own people!" Sometimes we feel like dirt, like useless garbage, but He desires to lift us up. God wants us to understand that we are *never* too used, too ugly, too divorced, too tempted, too raped, or too sheared of anything to belong with Him in the fold along with the other souls just like us.

When we return home, we enjoy the warmth inside the fold, and the Shepherd lifts us to the greatness He has destined for us. James 1:12 promises, "God blesses the people who patiently endure testing and temptation. Afterward they will receive the crown of life that God has promised to those who love him." This will be the ultimate Winners' Circle!

Chapter 49

VERY PRECIOUS

EIGHTY-FOUR AND USELESS! THIS IS HOW THE ELDERLY so often feel. Yet, they are individuals who, at one time, headed up large companies, led armies, raised families, or traveled the world. Now, even small tasks are overwhelming. Why should they continue on the journey?

As the Shepherd herded the sheep into the fold for the evening, He looked over the flock and saw a sheep moving slowly, struggling to reach Him. He left the others and went to the straggler—an elderly sheep that was unable to keep pace with the flock.

Bending down, the Shepherd encircled the sheep with His arms and said, "Don't be discouraged with your age, for you are very *precious* to me. You don't realize how your presence brings security and encouragement to the young sheep traveling with you. As they watch you, they see the continual, faithful care of the Shepherd." He walked the elderly sheep back to the fold, encouraging His loved one all the way.

Aching joints, hearing loss, crippled fingers, poor eyesight, restlessness, medications, and loneliness are some of the many issues that concern the elderly. Although their memories may fail them occasionally, they often recall a time when they were at the top of their game and their spoken words affected many lives and situations. Now they approach life each day with these memories, but the only question others ask them is, "How are you feeling today?"

It seems that the weighty questions and accolades are reserved for the young and the strong because of all that they have to offer. Perhaps Solomon was thinking along these lines when he penned, "The *instruction of the wise* is like a life-giving fountain; those who accept it avoid the snares of death" (Prov. 13:14). Seeking the advice and opinions of older, wise souls will not only enrich our lives, but, in turn, also enables them to be the valued advisors God intended them to be. It will help them to remember that they are very precious to Him.

Perhaps the Shepherd's tender embrace and words of comfort to the elderly sheep are a sufficient response to the cry of the aged writer in Psalm 71:18, "Now that I am old and gray, do not abandon me, O God. Let me proclaim your power to this new generation, your mighty miracles to all who come after me." The very existence of these dear ones and all that they represent—children, grandchildren, traditions, testimonies—are proof of God's faithfulness to those who follow Him. Through them, the young receive hope that they, too, will have families, homes, traditions, and the faithful care of the Shepherd.

Chapter 50

Intimate Moments

EVERYONE EXPERIENCES NIGHTS OF TOSSING AND turning, when sleep is elusive. It doesn't matter if worry, pain, or something unknown has caused the restlessness. The minutes stretch ever so slowly into hours of growing frustration. It is a very lonely, isolated feeling when everyone around us is resting and we are not. And at such a moment we should remember that Someone else is awake and longing for our company.

The flock was sleeping safely in the fold. One sheep, however, could not sleep, and it restlessly roamed the silent fold, occasionally resting or feeding. The Shepherd was sitting a distance away, very visible, but the sheep did not notice Him.

At last, completely exhausted and exasperated, the sheep became aware of the Shepherd and *went* to Him. He warmly received the sheep and welcomed the opportunity to share undisturbed moments together with it. In the early hours of the morning, calmed by the Shepherd's gentle touch, the weary sheep found rest.

The remarkable truth concerning our Shepherd is that He is always present—morning, noon, and night. Our need does not determine His whereabouts. However, our *focus* may determine our awareness of Him. When our thoughts are filled with what we do not have—in this scenario, restful sleep—we have little opportunity to enjoy what we do have, a loving God who longs for relationship with us. Just as God spoke to the heart of David, He speaks to us, "Come and talk with me." And just like David, our response should be, "LORD, I am coming" (Ps. 27:8).

Whether he was defending his nation on the battlefield or hiding from his enemies in the Judean wilderness, David experienced many troubled nights throughout his lifetime. However, he did not resort to counting sheep, for he knew just where to go during the long sleepless nights. "I lie awake thinking of you," he told God, "meditating on you through the night. Because you are my helper, I sing for joy in the shadow of your wings" (Ps. 63:6–7).

A restless night becomes a delightful opportunity to commune with our Lord. When no one is awake to interrupt our intimate moments with Him, we are free to read His Word or to express our words to Him. Worry, pain, and frustration are replaced with peace and rest. Even if we do not receive the sleep we so desire, we will be fit to travel when we start tomorrow's journey.

Chapter 51

SHARING SECRETS

SECRETS ARE HARD TO KEEP. WARS HAVE COMMENCED and friendships have been terminated with a slip of the tongue. When a secret has finally matured to the stage of exposure, we are generally selective in our choice of its beneficiary. We would hardly divulge its contents to the grocery checkout girl or shout it to the crossing guard. No, we would save it for that person who would listen to it with an intensity equal to our telling of it. We would share it with a close friend.

As the Shepherd sat on a rock and watched the grazing flock, a sheep came to Him, desiring His companionship. In an attempt to show its affection for the Shepherd, the sheep nuzzled His legs and nipped at His robe. The Shepherd loved this. With a hard tug, the sheep pulled the willing Shepherd to the ground, and they tumbled and played together. As they enjoyed the company of one another, the Shepherd shared secrets of rich pastures and safe journeys yet to come.

Many people have an intense desire to unlock past secrets and predictions for the future. In response to this, fortunetellers, psychic hotlines, and palm readers promise accurate readings and answers to life's problems all for a very small, persistent hook into our bank accounts. Although most are con artists, some possess information they have received through demonic activity that traps the eager seeker into a lifetime of dependence on evil lies.

God, of course, does not need the help of these charlatans to convey His secrets and promises. He prefers to share His truth with each individual directly, at precisely the right moment and in the right manner, through His Spirit living in us. Sometimes His direction and guidance for the future jump right out of the written pages of the Bible. He may bypass our senses and speak directly into our hearts with promises that only He knows will satisfy our longings. Occasionally, someone, some *godly* one, will speak a word from God to us—a word that is always in sync with God's written Word and confirms what He has done, is doing, or will do.

Although God never charges a *fee* for His secrets, there is usually a *cost*. Just as we would not share our secrets with strangers, neither does He. Psalm 25:14 teaches, "Friendship with God is reserved for those who reverence Him. With them alone He shares the *secrets* of His promises" (TLB, emphasis added). All friendships cost the time it takes to develop them, but the closer we grow to someone, the more intimately we share our hearts and our secrets.

The *fear*-based friendship of Psalm 25 is one that develops out of reverence and respect, not fright. Through a close relationship with God, we grow in our understanding of His covenant with us and learn to joyfully receive the hundreds of promises in His Word. The grazing sheep had to leave the benefits of the pasture and pursue its Shepherd to learn of the rich pastures and safe journeys that were ahead. It may have cost it the momentary pleasure of the pasture, but ultimately, it was a good deal.

Daniel, an Old Testament prophet, had an extraordinary friendship with God, and he once found himself as lion fodder because of it. However, it also spared his life and exposed a godless nation to the true and living God. When the wise men of Babylon, including captive Daniel and his Hebrew friends, were facing execution if they could not reiterate the king's dream and interpret it, Daniel and his friends asked God to reveal these secrets.

God did reveal the king's dream to Daniel, and he rejoiced, "Praise the name of God forever and ever.... He gives wisdom to the wise. . . . He reveals deep and mysterious things" (Dan. 2:20–22). Before he told the king his dream and interpreted it, Daniel explained to him, "There are no wise men, enchanters, magicians, or fortune-tellers who can reveal the king's secret. But there is a God in heaven who reveals secrets" (Dan. 2:27). Daniel's relationship with God may have cost him some tranquility on occasion, but ultimately, it was a good deal.

When we leave the busyness of our lives and the pleasures of this world for the company of the Lord, we are investing in a friendship that will result in secrets shared, His and ours. As we share our intimate thoughts and yearnings, He reveals His promises and deep mysteries, and that is a very good deal.

Chapter 52

THE ONE WHO COMPLETES US

YOU COMPLETE ME. YOU DID NOT BEGIN ME; YOU DID NOT carry me along the way; tomorrow you may be someone else; but for now, you complete me. Although this expresses a touching sentiment, it is an expectation that places a great deal of pressure on any relationship. In truth, there is really only One who possesses the ability to finish us, fulfill us and make us a whole person.

It was a beautiful day! The Shepherd settled Himself on grassy knoll, leaned back on a rock, and took in the surrounding beauty—a sun-drenched meadow, sweet breezes, birds, butterflies, and a babbling brook. The flock was scattered throughout the meadow, enjoying sweet grasses and the serenity of the day.

One sheep left the bountiful meadow and came to rest under the Shepherd's bent leg, at His thigh. As it was cuddling, nudging, and enjoying the safety and strength there, the Shepherd's hand came down to caress the attentive sheep. He was blessed by its choice to rest there rather than choosing all the other places available that day. The sheep, however, could think of no other place it would rather be. The Shepherd's thigh was such an intimate place.

Although a beautiful day and sweet grasses filled the sheep's senses, it was intimacy with the Shepherd that brought fulfillment to the sheep. So often we seek other people or things to fill a void that only the Shepherd can fill. We acquire, we achieve, and we conquer; yet we are filled with temporary fixes.

One man had it all—kingdoms, wealth, health, fame, and family. Yet he compared it all to chasing the wind, a fruitless effort to say the least. At the end of his life, Solomon wrote, "Here is my final conclusion: Fear God and obey his commands, for this is everyone's duty" (Eccles. 12:13).

Another man had very little of life's pleasures. For forty years he wore the same shoes, ate the same food, and owned no property. He spent much time away from home and family and had no one around to make him feel complete. Yet it was said of Moses, "There has never been another prophet…like Moses, *whom the Lord knew face to face*" (Deut. 34:10, emphasis added). Exodus 33:17 records, "And the Lord replied to Moses…'You have certainly found favor with me, and you are my *friend*'" (TLB, emphasis added). Moses was complete.

After Moses led the Israelites on a forty-year trek across the desert, God met him on Mount Nebo and showed him the Promised Land. However, He did not allow him to enter it because of a seemingly tiny infraction of His direction to bring forth much-needed water from a rock. Numbers 20:1–13 tells how Moses struck the rock instead of speaking to it, perhaps not realizing the ramifications of this. He had been instructed to strike a rock earlier in the journey as an example of the work of Christ. (See Exodus 17:6; 1 Corinthians 10:4.) To strike it again would imply that Christ, once crucified, is not enough.

Although this awesome servant of the Lord was not allowed to enter the Promised Land, he accepted this disappointment because his goal was *not* the Promised Land. His goal was the relationship he had with God on his way to the Promised Land, and he reached it. The Lord knew him face to face like no other. His reward was the Promised Land, and ultimately he received it in heaven, the eternal Promised Land.

Our striving for people and things is not the goal, for they were never intended to complete us. Instead, our goal is the relationship we have with the Lord along the way to our eternal reward. When we step away from the sweet grasses and the rest of the flock to find that intimate place with God under the protection of His thigh, we will discover, just like the sheep, that He is what we sought all along—the One who completes us.

NOTES

Chapter 10
No Worries

1. Corrie ten Boom quote, http://www.cybernation.com/quotationcenter/quoteshow.php?id=52571 (accessed November 13, 2007).

Chapter 26
Unreasonable Peace

1. Helen Lemmel, "Turn Your Eyes Upon Jesus," public domain.

Chapter 34
The Antidote to Panic

1. Notes from sermon by John Mason, www.freshword.com.

Chapter 37
A Name That Will Deliver

1. Napolean Bonaparte quote, http://www.brainyquote.com/quotes/authors/n/napoleon_bonaparte.html (accessed November 16, 2007).

Chapter 38
Victory Over Terror

1. George W. Bush, remarks made at prayer service at the Washington National Cathedral, September 15, 2001, http://query.nytimes.com/gst/fullpage.html?res=9503E5D71F38F936A2575AC0A9679C8B63&sec=&spon=&pagewanted=print (accessed November 16, 2007).

Chapter 47
He's Got Our Back

1. Mary C. Crowley quote, http://thinkexist.com/quotation/every_evening_i_turn_my_worries_over_to_god-he-s/214988.html (accessed November 20, 2007).

Chapter 48
Shear Humiliation

1. Seabiscuit, a champion thoroughbred horse, http://en.wikipedia.org/wiki/Seabiscuit (accessed November 20, 2007).

To Contact the Author

Do you have a story or question about the Shepherd's guidance through life's challenges? Phyllis welcomes your comments at www.shepherdmoments.com.